ON TRIAL

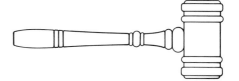

FAMOUS
MILITARY
TRIALS

ANDREW DAVID

Lerner Publications Company ▪ Minneapolis

ACKNOWLEDGMENTS: The illustrations are reproduced through the courtesy of: pp. 4, 36 (bottom), U. S. Air Force photo; p. 11, Huntington County Historical Society; pp. 13, 15 (left and right), 16, 19, 24, 33 (left and right), 36 (top), 38 (top, center, and bottom), 42, 45, 46, 74, 86, Library of Congress; p. 22, John F. Marszalek, *Court-Martial: A Black Man in America* (Charles Scribner's Sons, New York, 1972, p. 101); p. 25, *American Law Register;* pp. 26 (left and right), 27, U. S. Military Academy Archives, West Point, New York; p. 33 (center), Bureau of Engraving and Printing, Washington, D. C.; pp. 40, 69, 80, 93, 118, United Press International, Inc.; pp. 43 (top left), 63, The National Archives; p. 43 (bottom left), KSTP-TV, Minneapolis; p. 43 (right), U. S. Department of Defense photo; pp. 50, 51, U. S. Navy photo; pp. 52, 60 (Fort Leavenworth Public Information Service), 82, 84, U. S. Army photo; pp. 54, 55, Richard Whittingham, *Martial Justice, The Last Mass Execution in the United States* (Henry Regnery Publishing Company, Chicago, Illinois, 1971); p. 64, Richard P. Merrill; pp. 72, 77, 97, 103, 116, 117, Wide World Photos; p. 90, ABC News; p. 91, *Minnesota Daily;* p. 98, U. S. Marine Corps photo.

LIBRARY OF CONGRESS CATALOGING IN PUBLICATION DATA

David, Andrew.
Famous military trials.

(On Trial)
Includes index.
SUMMARY: Discusses eight trials in military courts involving military personnel, including Johnson Whittaker, Billy Mitchell, Eddie Slovik, and William L. Calley.

1. Trials (Military offenses)—United States—Juvenile literature. [1. Trials (Military offenses)] I. Title. II. Series.

KF7641.W5   343'.73'0143   79-17537
ISBN 0-8225-1428-3

Manufactured in the United States of America. Published simultaneously in Canada by J.M. Dent & Sons (Canada) Ltd., Don Mills, Ontario.

International Standard Book Number: 0-8225-1428-3
Library of Congress Catalog Card Number: 79-17537

2   3   4   5   6   7   8   9   10   85   84   83   82   81

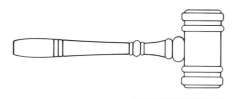

Contents

The 1925 trial of General Billy Mitchell *(standing)* was one of the most famous court-martials in American military history.

Introduction

While they are on active duty, the men and women of the United States armed forces live under a different law from that which civilians are subject to. This law is called "military law," and it is completely distinct from ordinary civil and criminal law. The military establishment has its own court system and its own code of laws, just as civilians have the federal and state court systems and the various federal and state laws.

Military law must be separate from civilian law because military life is regulated in a way that is very different from civilian life. Military life is based on strict discipline and a chain of command that must be obeyed. There are offenses in military life, therefore, that do not exist in civilian life. These can range from minor offenses, such as disrespect to an officer, to deadly serious offenses, such as desertion in wartime.

The military establishment is almost a world in itself. It even maintains responsibility for the conduct of its members in non-military offenses, such as murder, robbery, and other universal crimes. In rare instances, the civilian inhabitants of a country may even be subject to military law. But this situation only arises when military law is ordered by a government because of unusual circumstances that prevent civil law from functioning, such as revolution, civil war, or foreign invasion.

Under military law, a trial is called a "court-martial." It is conducted in many of the same ways that a civil trial is, but it also has certain important differences. There are three different types of courts-martial: summary, special, and general. The choice of which type will be used in each particular case will depend on the seriousness of the crime. A *summary court-martial* is used to try relatively minor cases. It cannot try officers, only enlisted men, and it cannot hand out punishments more severe than confinement for one month. The court-martial board, which decides the guilt or innocence of the accused, may consist of only a single officer.

A *special court-martial* is a tribunal that hears cases more serious than those heard at a summary court-martial. These are cases in which the punishment involved cannot exceed six months confinement or a "bad conduct discharge" (this is less serious than a "dishonorable discharge"). At a special court-martial, the prosecutor and the person representing the accused must be either lawyers or officers, and there must be at least three officers on the court-martial board.

A *general court-martial* hears the most serious cases that arise in military justice, and it can be convened by anyone from the president of the United States down to the commanding officer of a large military unit. A general court-martial has a presiding officer who is a military lawyer (sometimes called the "law officer" or the "law member") serving in the capacity of judge. The court-martial board, which acts as a jury, is composed of at least five or more military officers, each of whom must have a rank higher than that of the person on trial.

A general court-martial hears cases ranging from treason or desertion to simple assault and battery, as long as these cases are serious enough to involve a sentence of at least six months confinement or a dishonorable discharge. In extremely serious cases, the sentence may be as severe as the death penalty. The procedures used in a general court-martial are similar to those of an ordinary criminal trial. There is a pre-trial investigation before the court-martial itself is convened. The accused is provided a lawyer by the military (or he may hire a civilian lawyer at his own expense), and the prosecution is conducted by a military lawyer. All the cases described in this book were general courts-martial.

Military law has a process of appeal. Once a verdict is reached, it can be appealed for review to the commanding officer under whose jurisdiction the court-martial was held. Beyond that, the case may be appealed to a military board of review in Washington, composed of licensed lawyers. The final level of appeal is to the Court of Military Appeals, a high tribunal consisting of three civilian judges.

On the surface, military justice may not appear very different from ordinary civil justice. Over the years, however, it has been perhaps the most controversial of all forms of justice. Georges Clemenceau, the leader of France during World War I, once said that "military justice is to justice as military music is to music." In his view, military justice is regimented, limited, and not very creative. Many people share Clemenceau's feeling that military justice is inferior, and some say that it is positively unfair. They point out that the jury is appointed by the superior officer, who is the very person pressing charges against the accused. Therefore, the members of the jury might be inclined to carry out his wishes, for instance, by finding the accused guilty. Another problem is that the accused is not tried by his equals but rather by his superiors, often the very people against whom he is accused of having committed the crime. "It is," some people say, "like going on trial for having killed a child and finding that the judge was the child's father and the jury the child's relatives."

It is not the purpose of this book to determine whether military justice is fair or unfair. That is a question which each individual will have to decide for himself or herself. But as long as there is a military life that requires strict discipline and unchallenged obedience, there will probably always be a separate military law. And there will always be a need to strengthen it, modernize it, and keep it as fair and just as possible.

This book describes a number of famous military cases, each of which illustrates the workings of some aspect of military justice. The cases vary widely in their seriousness: there are members of the armed forces on trial for murder (Lieutenant Calley) as well as simply for "conduct unbecoming an officer" (Captain Levy). There is a general on trial (Billy Mitchell) as well as a private (Eddie Slovik). There is a civilian (Lambdin Milligan) as well as a group of prisoners of war (the Seven German Submariners). There are sentences that range from mass executions —

the largest for a single crime in the history of the United States — to simple suspension from duty for five years. There is seeming unfairness in one man spending two years in jail for speaking out against war crimes in Vietnam while another was simply confined to his apartment for three years, for having murdered 22 Vietnamese civilians in cold blood.

All the cases here are important in the history of military justice. Some have established guidelines for future cases, while others have left many vital questions unanswered. But each case is a fascinating story in itself. Together these cases paint a broad picture of the system of military justice and of those people who, for one reason or another, have come face to face with it.

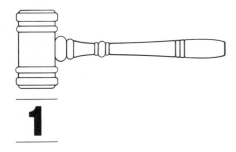

"Major General" Lambdin P. Milligan

On a bright autumn day in October 1864, a train backed slowly down the tracks of the Wabash railroad in Huntington, Indiana, about 90 miles northeast of Indianapolis. As it approached a house near the railroad tracks, the train came slowly to a stop. A squadron of soldiers, dressed in the dark blue uniforms of the Union Army, hurried out of one of the railroad cars and headed directly for the house, their rifles at the ready.

Inside the house was a tall, broad-shouldered man named Lambdin P. Milligan. Formerly, Milligan had been a teacher, but he was now a lawyer active in local politics. Although he looked strong and healthy, he was actually a very sick man. And he was not feeling at all well on that autumn day when the Union soldiers rushed into his house and put him under arrest.

At the time Milligan was arrested, the American Civil War had been going on for more than three years. The war had already taken more American lives than any

A drawing of Lambdin Milligan's house in Huntington, Indiana

previous war in American history. During the Civil War, Indiana was allied with the North, but the sympathies of many of the state's citizens were on the side of the South. In Indiana and other northern states, there were secret societies composed of people called "Copperheads," who were enthusiastic supporters of the Confederate cause. The Copperheads aided the South by spying, by encouraging and even helping Union soldiers to desert the Union Army, by propaganda campaigns, by sabotage, and by other terror tactics.

In July 1864, several months before the raid on Lambdin Milligan's house, a group of civilians had gathered outside a Union Army camp near Indianapolis. They were frightened, and they demanded to see the officer in charge,

Brigadier General Henry Carrington. The civilians claimed that various members of a Copperhead organization called the "Sons of Liberty" had approached them and demanded that they join the secret group and work for the South. The Copperheads had threatened to harm them if they did not cooperate, and these citizens wanted protection. When General Carrington agreed to help them, they revealed that the Sons of Liberty were also planning to seize the government arsenal in Indianapolis. If they succeeded, and if they received military assistance from the Confederacy, the Copperheads believed that they would then be able to capture the entire state of Indiana.

General Carrington asked who the members of this radical group were, and the people named some names, including that of "Major General" Lambdin P. Milligan. Milligan held the rank of "major general" in the Sons of Liberty, but he was not a real major general. In actual fact, he had no official rank, because he was not in the military forces of any established army. Milligan was a civilian, a Copperhead, and a member of the Sons of Liberty.

The attack on the Indianapolis arsenal never took place, although the Union forces were prepared for it. But General Carrington kept a record of what the civilians had told him, including the names of those who seemed to be involved.

During the rest of that spring and summer, things began going badly for the Confederate forces. By fall, the tide of battle had turned in favor of the Union. In October, a new officer named General Alvin Hovey took command of the Indiana military district. Hovey believed that the city of Indianapolis was filled with enemy officers and Southern sympathizers who were plotting treason and

General Alvin Hovey

that the entire state was in danger. As part of his defense against this threat, Hovey sent a group of his soldiers to the house of Lambdin Milligan, where they arrested him and took him off to the Union Army camp prison.

Milligan was charged with conspiracy to commit treason, giving aid to the enemy, and violating the laws of war. General Hovey appointed a military commission of officers from his own staff and brought Milligan to be tried by court-martial before them. But Milligan complained that the Army had no right to try him under military law because he was a civilian. General Hovey ignored Milligan's argument and conducted the court-martial anyway. Milligan was put on trial with three other Copperheads, although his lawyers had tried unsuccessfully to have him tried separately.

When the trial got under way, the judge advocate who

was prosecuting the four men described Milligan as "the right arm of this conspiracy in this state, the active, energetic and venomous leader. A man of unquestioned ability and determination; and with a heart full of hatred, envy and malice, he moved forward in this scheme of revolution with a coolness and intensity of purpose, not exceeded by another member of the conspiracy."

Although the evidence against them was strong, all four men had pleaded "not guilty." Midway through the trial, however, one of the defendants decided to change his plea to "guilty," in return for an offer of immunity from the judge advocate. He agreed to testify against his associates in return for a promise that he would not be prosecuted further if he did so. This defendant then testified against the remaining three defendants. Milligan and the other two were found guilty, and they were sentenced to be hanged. The date for the hanging was set for May 19, 1865, six months in the future.

At that point, Lambdin Milligan's lawyer went to Washington to plead his case directly before President Abraham Lincoln. He was received by the president but he was unsuccessful in his arguments on Milligan's behalf. President Lincoln upheld the authority of General Hovey to try Milligan under military law. The president did say, however, that if the war came to an end before the hanging took place, he might be able to commute Milligan's sentence and give him a prison term instead of executing him.

The Civil War ended in April 1865, but only five days later Abraham Lincoln was assassinated. Vice President Andrew Johnson became president, and he, of course, knew nothing of the private conversation that had taken place between Milligan's lawyer and President Lincoln.

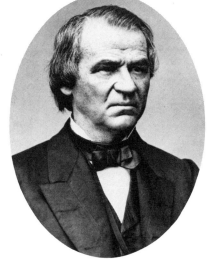

Abraham Lincoln   Andrew Johnson

Nine days before Milligan was scheduled to hang, his lawyer went before the circuit court of Indiana and asked for Milligan's release on the grounds that Milligan was being held in prison illegally. The circuit court judges could not reach a decision, and they referred the question to the United States Supreme Court, meanwhile postponing Milligan's execution. A month later, before the Supreme Court could consider the case, Milligan's sentence was commuted to life imprisonment by President Andrew Johnson.

While Johnson's act of mercy saved Milligan's life, it did not answer two important questions. First, had Lambdin Milligan been legally imprisoned? Second, did the armed forces have the right to try a civilian under military law? These were questions that the Supreme Court would have to decide.

Chief Justice Roger B. Taney

This was not the first time that a case of this kind had been brought before the courts. In the early days of the Civil War, a young civilian named John Merryman was arrested by the Union Army for "acts disloyal to the United States government." Merryman was imprisoned in an army camp, and his lawyer went directly to the chief justice of the Supreme Court in Washington to plead his client's case.

Roger B. Taney, the chief justice at that time, not only served on the Supreme Court but also sat as a circuit court judge in Baltimore, Maryland. (In this period of the nation's history, Supreme Court justices were also responsible for particular circuit court districts in which they heard cases.) In his capacity as circuit court judge, Taney heard Merryman's case and then issued a writ of *habeas corpus*, a legal document demanding that Merryman be brought to court so that the legality of his imprisonment could be determined. When the Union general holding Merryman refused repeatedly to bring his prisoner to court, Taney charged him with contempt of court.

Acting as chief justice of the Supreme Court, Taney wrote an opinion on the Merryman case, which was presented to President Abraham Lincoln. The chief justice explained that the general who had imprisoned Merryman claimed he had been authorized by the president to ignore a writ of *habeas corpus* in times of war or civil strife. But this was not possible, Taney noted, because, according to the Constitution, the right of *habeas corpus* could only be suspended by an act of Congress, not by a presidential order.

President Lincoln gave no answer to the chief justice's opinion. Instead, he went directly to Congress and asked that a law be passed giving the president the authority to suspend the writ of *habeas corpus* in a wartime situation. Congress obliged him by immediately passing such a law. There was nothing more that the chief justice could do, and John Merryman remained in prison.

The years passed, the war came to an end, and John Merryman was released from prison. But now Lambdin Milligan's case was going before the Supreme Court for a ruling on a subject very similar to the one that had been argued five years earlier. The Milligan case was important. At issue was the question of what would happen to the American system of justice if the armed forces had the power to arrest, imprison, and try civilians while suspending some of their constitutional rights at the same time. Who had the ultimate authority over civilians in time of war, the armed forces or the civil courts?

The case of Lambdin Milligan was officially brought before the Supreme Court on March 6, 1866. As lawyers on both sides of the issue presented their cases before the Court, Lambdin Milligan sat in a cell in a federal penitentiary in Ohio that he had become quite used to by now. The defense lawyers argued that Milligan had been denied a fair trial. The military had no right to imprison him nor to put him on trial; this should have been the responsibility of the civilian authorities. Because Milligan's trial had been illegal, they maintained, so were the findings and sentence of that trial.

The lawyers for the United States, on the other hand, argued that the trial had been completely legal. They pointed out that the president had the power to authorize the military to hold civilians in prison during wartime and to try them. Therefore, the military had lawfully carried out its duty. A state of war, they concluded, often required certain adjustments to be made in our system of justice, and this was a definite case in point.

The Supreme Court considered Lambdin Milligan's case for three weeks before delivering its opinion. The main question of this case, the Court said, was: "Has this [military] tribunal the legal power and authority to try and punish this man? . . . The importance of the main question . . . cannot be overstated; for it involves the very framework of the government and the fundamental prin-

Salmon P. Chase was chief justice of the Supreme Court when Lambdin Milligan's case was heard in March 1868.

ciples of American Liberty." Since the courts in Indiana were open and operating when Milligan was brought before a military commission, "no usage of war could sanction a military trial there for any offense whatever of a citizen in civil life. . . . One of the plainest constitutional provisions was, therefore, infringed when Milligan was tried by a court not ordained and established by Congress, and not composed of judges. . . ." Finally, Milligan had been denied another of his constitutional rights, said the Court, when he was not allowed a trial by jury.

But the Court made clear that its opinion did not question the government's power to proclaim martial law in situations of war or civil unrest. In instances such as a civil war or in the event of a foreign invasion, martial law could and should be proclaimed when the courts and the civil authorities are unable to function effectively. But it also said that martial law "cannot arise from a threatened invasion. The necessity must be actual and present . . . such as effectually closes the courts and deposes the civil administration. . . . Martial rule can never exist where the courts are open. . . ."

The courts had indeed been "open" in Indiana when Lambdin Milligan was arrested and tried in 1864. At that time, Indiana was not a battleground, and martial law should not have been substituted for civil law. The Supreme Court concluded that the military commission that had tried Milligan had been illegally constituted. Therefore, his conviction and sentence should be reversed.

Lambdin Milligan was not released from prison because he had been innocent but because his trial had been illegal. Some people said that it was wrong to release a man who had committed crimes as serious as treason. But a greater good had come from Milligan's case. From that day forward, the Supreme Court's ruling insured that all citizens would be guaranteed their basic constitutional rights to a fair trial even in time of war or national emergency, as long as the civil authorities were able to function. The Court's decision limited the powers of the military and upheld the rights of civilians and the greater authority of the civil laws that protect them in war as well as in peace.

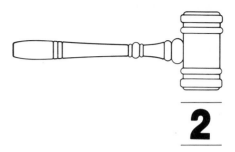

2

Cadet Johnson Whittaker

The United States Military Academy at West Point is located on a picturesque bluff overlooking the Hudson River, about 50 miles north of New York City. It is here that young cadets receive a college education and are trained to be officers in the United States Army. Many famous generals in American history, including Ulysses S. Grant, Robert E. Lee, John J. Pershing, Dwight D. Eisenhower, and Douglas MacArthur, have graduated from West Point. West Point was founded in 1802, and over the many years of its existence, a number of school traditions have developed. Some of those traditions were not at all pleasant, as a young cadet named Johnson Whittaker found out.

Johnson Whittaker was born in 1858, the son of a slave mother who worked on a large plantation in Camden, South Carolina. As a young boy, Johnson Whittaker lived on the plantation, and he saw it partially destroyed by the Union Army in the final days of the Civil War. As

Cadet Johnson Whittaker

time went on, however, he turned out to be more fortunate than most black children were in those days. He received a fairly good education and even began college in South Carolina. Then, at the age of 18, Whittaker was accepted as a cadet by the U.S. Military Academy. In 1876, he arrived at West Point full of fear, excitement, awe, and pride, eager to begin a new life that had opened up for him.

There was only one other black cadet at West Point at that time, and when Whittaker arrived, they became roommates. After a year, Whittaker's roommate became the first black to graduate from West Point in the Academy's history. Whittaker was left as the only black person at the school, and he was not assigned another roommate. Life was not easy for anyone at West Point, but for Whittaker it was especially difficult. One of the not-so-nice traditions at West Point was the "silent treatment." Because he was black, Whittaker was subjected to the "silent treatment," which meant that the white cadets would not socialize with him in any way and would speak to him only when they were required to for official reasons. As a result, Whittaker got no help or support from the other cadets in his studies, his military training, or his personal life.

Nevertheless, Johnson Whittaker managed to survive in this silent world for four years. But because he had been forced to repeat a year due to poor grades, Whittaker still had another year to complete at West Point. As his junior year was coming to a close, it looked as if he would pass into his senior year. But something changed all that. One morning in April 1880, Johnson Whittaker was discovered unconscious in his room, lying on the floor in a pool of blood. His hands and feet were bound and he was

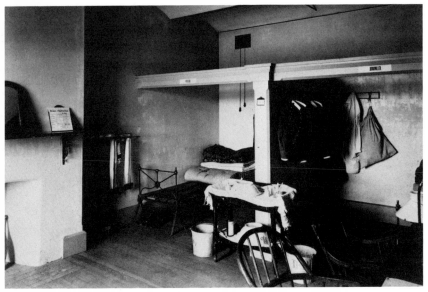

A typical West Point cadet's room in the 1880s

tied to the end of his bed. It looked as if he had been beaten and then slashed with a knife. The school doctor arrived and, after a few minutes, was able to revive Whittaker and get him up on his feet.

By this time, a few cadets and several officers had also arrived on the scene. One of them, Lieutenant Colonel Henry M. Lazalle, was the commandant in charge of cadets. General John M. Schofield, the superintendent of the academy, was on his way, because he wanted to take the situation under his personal control. In the meantime, the doctor was treating Whittaker's wounds, and both he and Colonel Lazelle were questioning the young cadet about what had happened.

Whittaker said that he had been awakened in the middle of the night to find three men, all wearing masks, standing over him. They knocked him out of bed and began beating him. Someone said, "Mark him like they do the pigs." The next thing Whittaker knew, his ears were being slashed. As he tried to protect himself, he was cut on his hand and foot. His assailants then tried to cut off his hair. Whittaker fought back, so they tied him to the foot of the bed. When the attackers had finished beating him and left, Whittaker tried to call for help, but, weak from the beating and from loss of blood, he passed out. The next thing he remembered, the doctor was reviving him.

Whittaker showed the officers a handwritten note that said he had received on the previous day. "Mr. Whittaker," the note said, "you will be fixed. Better keep awake." It was signed simply "A Friend."

A copy of the warning note received by Johnson Whittaker

Colonel Henry M. Lazalle   General John M. Schofield

General Schofield ordered Colonel Lazelle to conduct a full investigation of the incident, and the colonel began by questioning the doctor and many of the cadets. But no one wanted to believe that West Point cadets would inflict such a terrible beating on one of their own fellow students. Both the doctor and Colonel Lazelle believed that if the cadets would have done such a thing, it would only have been done in "the spirit of mere mischief." But all of the cadets quickly denied that they had anything to do with it. The colonel believed that his students would not be capable of committing such a dishonorable deed and then adding further dishonor by telling outright lies.

Therefore, when Colonel Lazelle wrote his report about the incident, he concluded that, for some unknown reason, Johnson Whittaker had written *himself* the threatening note, had beaten and slashed *himself,* and had then tied *himself* to the bed. Furthermore, because these acts were so unworthy of a West Point cadet, Colonel Lazelle recommended that Whittaker be given his choice of resigning, asking for a court of inquiry, or asking for a court-martial. When General Schofield confronted Whittaker with the results of Colonel Lazelle's investigation, the cadet insisted that the report was totally wrong, and he asked for a court of inquiry.

Three days after Johnson Whittaker had been found unconscious and bleeding on the floor of his room, he stood before a court inquiring into his case. A mathematics professor at West Point had been appointed to defend him.

Whittaker himself was the first witness in the case, and he was questioned in detail for a day and a half. He told his story well, reaffirmed it under cross-examination, and swore on the Bible that his version was true — that he had no part in the act which had been committed.

As the inquiry proceeded, the case of Johnson Whittaker attracted the attention of the nation's newspapers. Before long, it had become a controversial issue, and it eventually took on such political importance that Rutherford B. Hayes, then president of the United States, became involved in the case. President Hayes sent his own personal representative to West Point to attend the proceedings and see that the case was handled justly.

As the inquiry continued, dozens of witnesses were called, including officers, cadets, and civilians. Almost every witness disagreed with Whittaker's version of what had happened. Finally, after the inquiry had been in progress for about a month, Whittaker was called back to the witness stand. Again, he was asked detailed questions

The court of inquiry in the Whittaker case was held in the imposing Library Room at West Point.

about the beating, and again he answered exactly as he had before. At the end of the cross-examination, the prosecutor stepped back, eyed Whittaker with suspicion, and asked him whether he had, in fact, written the note of warning.

"I did not," said Whittaker.

"Then why have the handwriting experts agreed that you did write the note?"

"I don't know," Whittaker answered.

The opinions of these "experts" had been submitted as

evidence, but they had not explained how they arrived at this conclusion. After the cross-examination concerning the note, the court of inquiry came to a close.

The prosecutor summed up his case, bitterly attacking Whittaker's testimony and defending the honor of the other West Point cadets. The evidence against Whittaker was only circumstantial; that is, it was not direct or first-hand evidence. According to the prosecutor, however, it was strong enough to warrant a finding of guilty. "The circumstantial evidence against [Cadet Whittaker] is so strong," he concluded, "that the merits of the case stringently demand that he be tried by a General Court Martial . . . for conduct unbecoming a Cadet and a gentleman, and for perjury."

The members of the court agreed, and Whittaker was found guilty. But neither West Point, the Army, nor the president wanted to take any action against Johnson Whittaker. The country as a whole was not convinced of his guilt, and the issue was argued back and forth in the newspapers.

In June, Whittaker took his final examination in philosophy, the course with which he had been having the most trouble. Several days later, he was informed that he had failed the exam. Months dragged by, but still nothing was done to resolve Whittaker's case. For the time being, he remained a cadet, at least officially. In the end, Johnson Whittaker was quietly given an extended leave of absence from the United States Military Academy at West Point. General Schofield was transferred to another post. Then, just before Christmas of 1880, President Hayes announced that a full court-martial had been scheduled, to begin after the first of the year.

A full court-martial was something that not only Whittaker but also the officers and cadets of West Point had wanted. Whittaker wanted it so that he could prove his innocence and be reinstated to the military academy. The others wanted it to prove that the incident cast no blame on any person associated with West Point except Johnson Whittaker.

The court-martial began in New York City on January 20, 1881. Ten officers, most of whom had never attended West Point, were appointed to hear the case. The board was designed to be impartial, and the court-martial would be held in a courtroom away from West Point, so that no matter what the outcome, there would be no charges of prejudice. This time, Whittaker was to have professional legal assistance; Daniel H. Chamberlain, a former governor of South Carolina and a respected attorney, was appointed Whittaker's defense counsel. As the court-martial began, Johnson Whittaker appeared in court in his cadet uniform and was asked how he would plead. "Not guilty," he replied in a clear and forceful tone.

Among the first witnesses to be called to testify was General Schofield himself. The general spoke of the honor among West Point cadets, and he insisted that it was almost impossible to imagine that cadets would carry out such an act and then deny it under oath. General Schofield also admitted that he had originally believed that Whittaker had been attacked, but that he had changed his mind later. "Well," said the general, "I began to think after a while that [Whittaker] was too ready in his demand for a court of inquiry. It seemed to me . . . that he had known what was coming and that he was assured of a strong backing if he got in trouble."

But Whittaker had a good defense attorney. He thought that the General's line of reasoning was incredible, and he quickly brought that fact to the attention of the court-martial board. "Do you think that a demand for a court of inquiry was a sign of guilt?" the attorney asked, in a tone of disbelief. The general admitted that he did. Defense attorney Chamberlain then went on to accuse General Schofield of a prejudiced attitude on the subject of Whittaker's guilt or innocence. Furthermore, he pointed out that this prejudice had undoubtedly influenced the court of inquiry that had been convened under his command.

The court-martial dragged on and on. Weeks after it began, a new president, James A. Garfield, took office and was informed of the progress of the case. Many cadets were called to the witness stand to tell their stories, and all those who testified believed that Whittaker had hurt himself for his own personal reasons. Each cadet defended the "silent treatment," arguing that there was nothing wrong with it and that it had no bearing on the act that was under investigation. The West Point doctor who had originally treated Whittaker's wounds also expressed his strong belief that Whittaker was guilty. But another doctor, who had also examined Whittaker, testified that ". . . upon reflection I made up my mind that he had not done it — could not have done as brutal a thing." Handwriting experts also testified, some saying that Whittaker had written the warning note and others saying that he had not.

As the court-martial progressed, things began going a little more in Whitaker's favor than they had earlier at the court of inquiry. Several witnesses testified that Whittaker's hands had been tied very tightly, and this created some doubt as to whether he could have possibly tied himself up so effectively. On the whole, there was little evidence to show that "others" had committed the act, but there was even less evidence that Johnson Whittaker had done it himself.

When it was time for the defense to present its case, Whittaker was called to the witness stand again. He repeated his version of the story and was then cross-examined by the prosecution. Whittaker stuck to his story, but now and then he did contradict himself on minor points. On the whole, however, Johnson Whittaker was a good witness in his own defense. The prosecution had made a point of stressing the honor and integrity of the West Point cadets. For his part, the defense attorney also called numerous witnesses to testify to Whittaker's good character.

For months the arguments went back and forth. The court-martial, which had begun in January, had now lasted through the first half of May. Finally, on May 17, 1881, both sides ended their cases, and the attorneys presented their closing arguments. On June 10, 1881, nearly five months from the day the court-martial had begun, the board reached its verdict. They found Johnson Whittaker guilty both of mutilating himself and of perjuring himself before the court of inquiry that had been previously conducted at West Point. The board sentenced Whittaker to a dishonorable discharge from the military academy, to a year's imprisonment, and to a fine of one dollar.

Before the sentence could be carried out, however, there was first to be a review of Whittaker's case by the Judge Advocate General's office in Washington. In December of

Three American presidents — Rutherford B. Hayes *(left)*, James A. Garfield, and Chester A. Arthur *(right)* — were involved in the court-martial of Johnson Whittaker. President Arthur overturned Whittaker's conviction in March 1882.

that year, D. G. Swain, the judge advocate general, presented the result of his review to the secretary of war. In his opinion, the verdict of the court-martial board had been totally wrong and should be reversed. Swain not only picked apart the prosecution's case, but he also argued that the court-martial itself had not been legal because President Hayes, who had ordered it, did not, in fact, have the right to do so. The report of the judge advocate general passed from the secretary of war to the attorney general and finally to the president. James Garfield had been assassinated earlier that year, and the new president, Chester A. Arthur, received the report in March 1882. President Arthur overturned the conviction of Johnson Whittaker on the grounds that the court-martial itself had been illegal. He did not, however, offer an opinion as to whether Whittaker was guilty or innocent.

On the day that Johnson Whittaker learned that his conviction had been overturned, he also received word that he had been formally discharged from the U.S. Military Academy because he had failed that philosophy course almost two years before. Johnson Whittaker went back to South Carolina. He finished his education there and went on to become a lawyer, a teacher, and a school administrator. He married, and the Whittakers had two sons. When the Whittaker boys were grown, they both received commissions in the United States Army and served as officers in World War I. Johnson Whittaker died in 1931 at the age of 72, his body — and, no doubt, his heart as well — still bearing the scars he had received that night at West Point so many years ago.

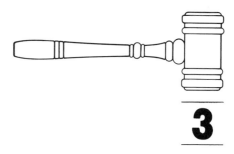

General Billy Mitchell

A small fleet of heavily armored German warships rolled with the sea in the waters of the Atlantic Ocean, just off the coast of Norfolk, Virginia. There was a U-boat (one of the devastating German submarines), a destroyer, a cruiser, and the *Ostfriesland*, one of Germany's most powerful battleships, a vessel so strongly built that many said it was absolutely unsinkable. Suddenly, a force of small biplanes appeared in the skies, struggling and weaving under heavy loads of bombs. One by one, the planes headed for the German warships.

The attack of the small planes was not an act of war. The time was June 1921, and World War I had been over for three years. Germany no longer even *had* a military force. The bomb-laden airplanes were being used in a kind of experiment. The ships, which had been captured from the German Navy, were actually a "ghost fleet": their engines were shut down and there was not a man aboard any of them.

General Mitchell directed the attack on the German warships from his own airplane.

General Billy Mitchell

The demonstration was being staged by Brigadier General Billy Mitchell, the most successful American air commander of World War I. General Mitchell had been the first officer to command planes that actually took part in combat. Until then, air power had only been used for scouting, spying, and other non-combat missions. General Mitchell's planes had been quite successful in the war effort, yet after the war was over, the air corps was still only a minor subdivision of the Army. Its planes were thin-skinned, wobbly, and small. The air corps was simply not considered very important by either the Army or the Navy. General Billy Mitchell, who was much more of an "airman" than an "Army man," did not share this opinion at all. He believed that the air corps was not simply an important fighting unit but that, in the future, it was going to be the *most* important military force.

After the war, Mitchell went before Congress and explained that air power was even greater than sea power, because airplanes could sink any naval ship by bombing it. High-ranking officers of the Navy ridiculed him for this statement. Josephus Daniels, secretary of the Navy, boasted that he would not be afraid to "stand bareheaded on the deck of a battleship and let Brigadier General Mitchell take a crack at me with a bombing airplane." Mitchell replied that he could prove his statement if he had some ships to bomb. So the captured German ships were provided as targets, and the test was arranged.

General Mitchell himself directed the attack on the German warships from his own plane, while other military leaders, government officials, and various congressmen watched from the shore. Millions of other people throughout the United States were also awaiting the outcome of

The sinking of the German battleship *Ostfriesland*

the test. General Billy Mitchell's operation had by now become a topic of great national interest. After Mitchell's planes arrived at the target area, they dove to the attack. One after the other, the small biplanes unleashed their bombs at the ships. First, the submarine went under, then the destroyer and the cruiser keeled over and sank. Finally the mighty German battleship *Ostfriesland,* brutally damaged, raised its bow to the sky and, like a great broad-blade sword, slid into the sea.

The officers and officials of the Navy Department were stunned. General Mitchell had proven the might of air power beyond their expectations. But still they refused to give in. While they had to admit that airplanes could sink unarmed, unmanned ships anchored at sea, they believed that fully armed ships under the command of naval officers and experienced sailors would produce a completely different outcome. In a fair fight, they insisted, Billy Mitchell's air power would be soundly defeated.

The congressmen and government officials in Washington seemed to think that the Navy's argument had been correct. It appeared that Mitchell had not won the dispute, in spite of the success of his experiment. As time went on, nothing was done to enlarge or modernize the air corps, but General Mitchell refused to give up. He continued to take his case for a strong and separate air force to both the government and the people of the United States. But the officials of the Department of War grew tired of Mitchell's campaign, and they transferred him to San Antonio, Texas.

Four years passed. Then several air tragedies occurred that shocked the nation. The worst of these tragedies involved a Navy dirigible named the *Shenandoah,* which

The Navy dirigible *Shenandoah* after its crash in 1925

had been caught in a severe storm. The ship was torn in half, and many members of its crew fell thousands of feet to their deaths; 14 men died in the accident. Word leaked out that the airship might not have been in a safe flying condition but that the Navy had ordered it to be flown anyway. The Navy ignored this rumor and announced instead that the bright side of the accident was that it showed clearly that we had little to fear from an "airborne enemy." Flying craft could not even weather a storm, said the Navy. How could it survive an attack by the anti-aircraft guns of a Navy ship?

This was too much for General Billy Mitchell. He conducted his own investigation of the accident itself and then held a press conference in San Antonio where he announced that the accidents were a "direct result of incompetency, criminal negligence, and almost treasonable administration by the War and Navy Departments." General Mitchell was back on the front pages of almost every major newspaper in the United States. His statement was powerful and shocking, one that the average military officer would not dare to make in public about his superiors. Military officials were horrified, but at the same time, they were pleased. Now they had a *real* offense with which to get back at their long-time critic.

Billy Mitchell had expected his superiors to react as they did, and he was prepared for trouble. As he had anticipated, he was soon ordered to stand trial before a general court-martial. His first act was to engage Frank R. Reid, a civilian attorney, to represent him as defense counsel. No less than eight charges were placed against Mitchell, all expressing the ideas that his statement had been damaging to good order (and to proper military discipline) and that his conduct was "of a nature to bring discredit upon military service. . . ." The court-martial consisted of four other major generals and six brigadier generals. One member of the board was 45-year-old Major General Douglas MacArthur, a personal friend of Mitchell's.

The court-martial began on October 28, 1925, in Washington, D.C., with Major General Charles P. Summerall presiding. As one of his first acts, Mitchell's lawyer challenged not only two members of the board but also the presiding officer, General Summerall himself. He

General Billy Mitchell *(standing, left)* listens as the charges against him are read.

charged that these officers were prejudiced against Mitchell, and he was successful in having all three of them removed from the court-martial board.

The court-martial of Billy Mitchell had attracted the attention of the entire country, and several prominent persons from many walks of life were scheduled to take part. The prosecution would put the famous explorer Admiral Richard Byrd on the stand, while the defense planned to call Eddie Rickenbacker, World War I's greatest American pilot; the fiery congressman Fiorello LaGuardia (later to become one of New York City's most famous mayors); and Will Rogers, the nation's most popular comedian, to testify on Billy Mitchell's behalf.

The prosecution's task was simple. No one denied that

Richard Byrd

Eddie Rickenbacker

Will Rogers

General Mitchell had made the shocking and critical statements attributed to him. In fact, Mitchell himself readily admitted it. Since all the charges against him stemmed from those statements, the main thrust of the trial would be the defense's efforts to show that Mitchell had been correct and that his criticism of the War Department officials had been fair and just.

Defense Attorney Reid stated at the very beginning that he intended to show that Mitchell's statements were *true,* and that they could not be considered "libelous" on two other grounds. First, the statements were directed at the War Department, not at an individual, and libel cannot be committed against a non-living thing. And second, officers have the right to enjoy the freedom of speech guaranteed under Article I of the U.S. Constitution, so long as they do not use this freedom to violate national security. Then, Reid announced that he intended to call more than 70 witnesses to the stand, in order to prove that General Billy Mitchell was innocent. Everyone prepared for a very long trial.

One of the first witnesses called by the defense was the wife of the captain of the *Shenandoah,* the Navy dirigible that had been destroyed in a storm. She testified that her husband had been unwilling to fly the dirigible because he believed it was not in safe condition. He had expressed his fears and objections to his superiors, but they ordered him to fly the mission anyway. Being a good officer, the captain had obeyed his orders. This was startling testimony, because the secretary of the Navy had previously told reporters that the captain had made *no* protest at all. The captain's wife added that a Navy representative had been to see her only a short while earlier and had pre-

The court-martial board hears the testimony of Mrs. Zachary Lansdowne, the wife of the captain of the *Shenandoah*.

sented her with a written statement that they wanted her to make, a statement that upheld the Navy's side of the story. By revealing the Navy's effort to control her testimony, she made her appearance in court even more damaging to the Navy.

Next to tesify was a long series of air corps officers. They expressed their belief in the importance of air power for the future security of the United States, the Army's overwhelming lack of interest in this power, and the terribly poor situation into which the air corps had been allowed to degenerate. Now, what seemed to be on trial was the government's entire policy of national defense, and the individual named Billy Mitchell seemed almost forgotten. The questions came and went. Which was more valuable in defense, a navy or an air force? Which could harm an enemy more: being bombed by airplanes or being shot at by the artillery and the infantry? Was it really true that the airplane was "shrinking" the world, and that other forms of transportation, like the ship, would take a back seat because of this? In 1925, this last question was difficult to answer. Charles Lindbergh's historic non-stop flight across the Atlantic was still another year and a half in the future.

Finally, General Billy Mitchell himself took the stand. He described the great potential that he envisioned for an air force in the nation's defense. He told of the endless difficulties he had experienced in attempting to further the cause of a United States air force. He described how the air corps of the day was not simply at a standstill but was actually deteriorating. And he explained why he believed that the United States could be properly defended only if it had an air force provided with the proper equipment and manpower.

Then Mitchell was cross-examined by the prosecuting attorney. The prosecution wanted to show that Mitchell was describing not *facts* but merely opinions and that his statements were only prophecies that might — or might not — come true. The prosecutor tried desperately to make General Mitchell appear eccentric, an oddball like those people who wander the streets preaching that the world will end tomorrow. This was not the kind of man the military needed for the task of defending the nation, said the prosecution. Dreamers, screwballs, and fanatics were not the type of people who should determine the defense policy of the United States. This was not, of course, the issue that was supposed to be decided at the trial. But then, neither was the matter of American defense policy, which Mitchell and his lawyer had introduced. According to the law, the central issue of the trial should have been simply whether Billy Mitchell was guilty or innocent of the charges against him.

From the outset of the trial, the defense had had serious problems. The generals sitting in judgment at the court-martial believed that, under the existing policies of the armed forces, Mitchell should not have made those statements, and under no circumstances should he have criticized his superiors in public. Such behavior was considered dishonorable and disgraceful in military life. Whether his motivation was right or not or whether his remarks were correct or incorrect was, in their view, beside the point. After all their many years of training and military discipline, the officers believed that Billy Mitchell simply should not have said what he did.

When the court-martial came to a close, the generals met in private to decide the question of Billy Mitchell's guilt or innocence. Not surprisingly, they found him guilty as charged. General Billy Mitchell was suspended from the Army for five years.

As a civilian, Billy Mitchell continued to campaign vigorously for an effective air force. Although he was never allowed to re-enter the Army, he saw the U.S. Air Force grow, although quite slowly, during the early 1930s. In February 1936, 10 years after he had left the Army, Billy Mitchell died. He had recognized the importance of air power in modern warfare and had correctly predicted that it would become the most powerful weapon yet devised. And he even predicted that the United States Navy would one day be in serious danger of air attack.

The ten generals who found Billy Mitchell guilty. Major General Douglas MacArthur is the fourth from the left.

Less than six years after Billy Mitchell died, the Japanese successfully bombed the Navy ships at Pearl Harbor, an act that crippled the nation's Pacific fleet and led to America's entry into World War II.

Billy Mitchell did not live to see many of his predictions come true, but no one today questions the importance of air power. Pearl Harbor, the German *Blitzkrieg*, the Allied bombings of Europe, the atomic bombs dropped on Hiroshima and Nagasaki, and the immense use of air power in Korea and Vietnam all testify to the significance of air power in modern warfare. Although Billy Mitchell was found guilty, we know today that what he said was correct and that those who brought him to trial, and those who testified against him, were proved wrong by the events of history.

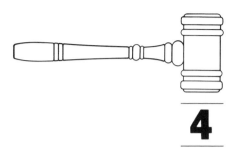

The Seven German Submariners

World War II was raging in both Europe and Asia in June 1943. One warm afternoon during that month, a German submarine, the U-118, was slowly cruising on the surface of the Atlantic, not far from the Azores Islands. Everything seemed peaceful, and several young sailors were sunbathing on the deck of the sub.

Suddenly, two American planes appeared in the sky. The startled German sailors raced to the hatch and dropped down inside the ship. With sirens blaring, the submarine dove for cover beneath the water's surface, but it was too late. Underwater bombs called "depth charges," dropped from the planes, exploded in the sea all around the sub, severely damaging it. The captain gave the order to surface. Some of the sailors hoped to fight off the planes with their machine guns on deck, but as they rushed out of the hatches, they came face to face with the machine guns of the American planes.

Among the German sailors who climbed out on deck

The German U-18 under attack by American planes. Two of its crew can be seen about to escape from the damaged submarine.

was a man named Werner Drechsler. He had not been on deck for more than a few seconds before he was wounded in both the neck and the knee. But Drechsler managed to get off the sinking boat. As he swam away, the submarine went down in a dazzling fountain of spray and debris. Only 16 members of the boat's 58-man crew survived. They were picked up later by an American destroyer and taken as prisoners of war.

New prisoners of war were taken first to Fort Meade in Maryland for intensive questioning. Then, usually within a few days, they were sent on to permanent prisoner-of-war camps elsewhere in the United States. But Werner

Werner Drechsler *(left)* arrives at the U.S. naval base at Norfolk, Virginia. After being processed as a prisoner of war, he was sent to Fort Meade for interrogation.

Drechsler was not sent to another camp because, while he was being questioned by U.S. naval officers, he decided to cooperate with them. Drechsler stayed on at Fort Meade, helping American officers to interrogate other German submariners who were brought there as prisoners.

At the end of nine months, the Navy decided they no longer needed Werner Drechsler. So they turned him over to the Army, which was responsible for operating all prisoner-of-war camps in the United States. The Navy warned the Army not to place Drechsler in a prisoner-of-war (POW) camp with other German submariners, because he would be recognized and branded a traitor. But

51

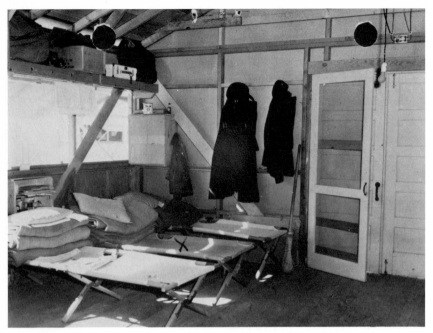

The bunk assigned to Werner Dreschler in the barracks at Papago Park in Arizona

for some unknown reason, the Army not only ignored this advice but actually sent Drechsler to a POW camp at Papago Park, Arizona, that housed almost all the other German submariners imprisoned in the United States.

Werner Drechsler arrived at Papago Park at about 3:00 p.m. on the afternoon of March 12, 1944. Six hours later, badly beaten, Werner Drechsler was hanged by his fellow prisoners from a rafter in one of the camp's shower rooms.

The next morning, the prisoners at Papago Park were questioned about the murder, but each man claimed he had neither heard nor seen anything on the previous night. Over the next few weeks, several hundred prisoners at the camp were questioned. Among these was Captain

Jurgen Wattenburg, the highest ranking German naval officer in the camp. Wattenburg had been the commander of a submarine and, before that, the executive officer of the famous German battleship *Graf Spee.* He was asked if he knew anything about the murder of Drechsler. "I don't know," he coldly replied, "whether he was killed or whether he killed himself." And that was about as much information as the American officers could get out of any of the prisoners questioned at Papago Park. But the Army persisted. After questioning the prisoners for weeks, they brought in a lie-detector expert to help, and more than 125 prisoners were given lie-detector tests. This type of interrogation went on for over a month, and the Army narrowed their investigation to a list of 20 top suspects.

The Army decided to take these 20 suspects to a secret camp at Stockton, California, for further questioning. Most of the 20 German suspects were enlisted men, equal in rank to Army privates, but there were several non-commissioned officers in the group as well. The prisoners were questioned continually for a month at the secret camp. The "methods" of questioning used at the camp were classified "for security reasons," and they have never been fully revealed. But it is safe to assume that they were not gentle methods. In the end, however, they *were* effective, and one of the noncommissioned officers, Friedrich Murza, broke down and began to tell the entire story in detail.

Murza said that after Drechsler's identity was discovered, a number of prisoners had met to discuss what to do with him. All agreed that Drechsler was a traitor and should be punished. "I said the man should be beaten up,"

Murza said. According to Murza's testimony, however, the group decided to murder Drechsler. A number of low-ranking enlisted men then entered Drechsler's barracks, beat him, and dragged him outside. When an Army jeep drove by just outside the fence, the prisoners ran off. Drechsler screamed for help, but the American guards did not respond. Later, the prisoners returned to Drechsler's barracks, beat him again, and then carried his unconscious body to the shower room, where they hanged him.

Murza began to name names, and so did Siegfried Elser, another noncommissioned officer. The case was broken, and the Army investigators decided to concentrate on seven low-ranking enlisted men, who ranged in age from 20 to 25 years old. Their names were Helmut Fischer, Fritz Franke, Bernhard Reyak, Guenther Kuelsen, Otto Stengel, Heinrich Ludwig, and Rolf Wizuy. The Army confronted the men with the fact that it now knew the whole story, and each of the seven admitted his role in the slaying. Each man then wrote a statement of confession, describing the act, the events that led up to it, and the reasons for having carried it out. But to each of the young Germans it had only been an *act,* not a crime. In fact, each man stated that he was actually carrying out his patriotic duty by punishing a traitor and preventing him from doing further harm to the German nation. The seven men were doing exactly what would have been expected of American prisoners of war faced with a similar situation.

The U.S. Army did not agree, however, and all seven men were charged with murder in the first degree. Murza and Elser, the two noncommissioned officers who had revealed the truth to Army interrogators, were charged only with having "aided, assisted, counseled and advised the above-named murderers . . . and therefore should be charged and tried as accessories before the fact." Before the seven German sailors could be tried, they needed time to recover from the nearly three months of "questioning" they had undergone. Three of the seven had to be sent to Army hospitals, while the other four were treated in a rehabilitation center. Finally, in July 1944, a general court-martial was ordered. Twelve Army officers were appointed to the court-martial board, to serve in the basic capacity of a jury. One defense attorney and an assistant were appointed to represent all seven men. Each man was charged with the "willful and premeditated murder of Prisoner of War Werner Drechsler." The charges against the two noncommissioned officers, however, were dropped completely.

On August 15, 1944, in Florence, Arizona, the seven young Germans stood before the president of the court-martial board. "How do you plead to the charge?" he asked each one in turn.

"Not guilty," each man answered.

The prosecution planned to base its case on the confessions that had been written and signed by the seven defendants. The court-martial, however, began with the calling of witnesses. Perhaps the only thing that was notable in this early testimony was a statement by the colonel who had been in charge of the original investigation. He testified that some of the methods of interrogation used at the secret camp at Stockton might have involved the use of force. Then the statements of the seven Germans were read to the court-martial board, one additional witness was called, and the prosecution rested its case.

Otto Stengel

Helmut Fischer

Bernhard Reyak

Fritz Franke

Guenther Kuelsen

Heinrich Ludwig

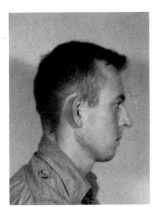

Bernhard Reyak

Rolf Wizuy

Major Taylor then presented the case for the defense. He asked Captain Oscar Schmidt, the chief interrogator from the secret camp at Stockton, to take the stand. Major Taylor asked the witness if a gas mask had been used during the questioning of Otto Stengel.

"Yes," answered Captain Schmidt.

"Did you use a method that involved the use of an overcoat?"

"I think I did see an overcoat," Schmidt replied.

"How was use made of the gas mask?" Taylor continued.

"It was put on his head and face and used in the ordinary manner," said Schmidt.

"Was an onion used in the gas mask?"

"There was."

The defense then called several of the German sailors to give their version of the interrogation. The defendants could testify in one of two ways: under oath (which meant they could be cross-examined by the prosecution) or in the form of "unsworn statements." These statements would not be subject to cross-examination, but they did not qualify as legal evidence either, and there was nothing to require the court to believe what was stated. The seven decided to testify with unsworn statements.

Otto Stengel was the first of the Germans to take the stand. He testified that at first he was given nothing to eat at Stockton and was taken for wild automobile rides into the countryside, in the hope that he would be frightened into confessing. Stengel said that he was suffering from appendicitis at that time, but that he received no medical treatment until after he confessed. During the questioning, Stengel reported, "three heavy coats were put on my shoulders and someone opened the steam heat. My shirt and underwear were torn and my sex organs were hanging out, at which time I was pushed toward the steam heat and burned myself." A gas mask was put on Stengel's face, and "an onion and garlic were smashed and put into the gas mask. . . . Then the American lieutenant stepped next to me and closed the inlet holes of the gas mask . . . to find out how long I could stand without air. . . . When he had done this with me about eight times, I collapsed unconscious."

Helmut Fischer was the next witness. "I had to cross my arms under the seat of my pants," he explained. "Captain Schmidt stepped twice with his shoes on my crossed hands. . . . [By the time] they left me alone at 7:00, I was in such [serious] physical condition that my whole body was shaking." Major Taylor then asked Fischer if he had been advised of his rights before the interrogation he had just described. Fischer said that he had not.

The last witness was Rolf Wizuy. He testified that he had been taken for automobile rides similar to those given to Stengel, that he had been kicked by Captain Schmidt, and that he had not been allowed to sleep for several days. Major Taylor called no other witnesses, basing the case for the defense primarily on the fact that the confessions had not been obtained by legal methods.

At this point, the court-martial of the seven men for first-degree murder was virtually over. The entire proceedings had taken less than two hours. The lawyers presented their closing arguments, and then all 12 members of the court-martial board retired to consider their decision. A short while later, they returned to the courtroom,

The U.S. Disciplinary Barracks at Fort Leavenworth, Kansas. The seven German submariners were held in the large building at the top of the picture.

and each officer handed a piece of paper to the president of the court-martial board. After looking at all the pieces of paper containing the findings of the jurists, the colonel announced that the board had reached a unanimous decision. "The court," he said, "finds the accused guilty . . . (and) sentences the accused . . . to be hanged by the neck until dead."

This was not the end of the case, however; there was a definite procedure to be followed for reviewing all court-martials involving capital punishment. While the review was taking place, the seven Germans would be held in the Army prison at Fort Leavenworth, Kansas. The first step in the review procedure was to submit the case to Major General William E. Shedd, under whose command the court-martial had taken place. In September 1944, General Shedd announced that he approved of the findings and sentences, but he added a recommendation that the sentences be commuted to life imprisonment.

The next step in the appeal process was to present the case to a board of review that met regularly at Fort Douglas, Utah. This board reviewed all aspects of the court-martial, its findings, and the sentences that resulted from it. In November 1944, the review board reached its decision. It not only agreed that the prisoners were guilty but also decided *not* to accept General Shedd's recommendation to commute the death sentences to life imprisonment. All findings and recommendations in the case were then sent to the office of the secretary of war in Washington to be reviewed and, finally, presented to the president himself for confirmation.

At this point, the case of the seven German submariners began to take on a new significance. The United

States, which had pledged to abide by the rules of the Geneva Convention, was required to inform the German government of any prisoners who were sentenced to be executed. Late in 1944, the U.S. government provided the Germans with all records and information relating to the trial and reviews, basically to prove that there was legal justification to carry out the executions.

In January 1945, the German government replied that they had a number of American prisoners of war who had also been sentenced to death. The German government suggested that Germany and the United States might like to consider an exchange of prisoners rather than both proceeding to carry out their proposed executions of each other's citizens.

The United States agreed to consider this, and negotiations for the prisoner exchange were begun. There was, however, a problem of communication. Although the United States and Germany were at war, they had been able to communicate through the government of Switzerland, which had remained strictly neutral during the war. But now, the United States and England were invading Germany from the west and the Russians were surging in from the east. Germany was in chaos, and communication with those in authority was very difficult.

Finally, after much delay, a plan was drawn up that seemed to be agreeable to both countries. The seven German submariners would be turned over to Swiss authorities at the Swiss-French border. At the same time, the American prisoners would be turned over at the Swiss-German border. Unfortunately, the negotiations could not be completed speedily enough. Before the exchange could be made, Germany surrendered. Back in Washing-

On August 23, 1945, President Harry S Truman confirmed the decision to execute the seven German prisoners.

ton, Army officials received the news that the American soldiers who were to be exchanged had been safely recovered. With this in mind, the provost marshall general at the Department of War recommended that, because there was no longer any need for an exchange, the death sentences of the seven Germans should be carried out.

The case was then sent to President Harry S Truman for review and confirmation. His decision was announced on the night of August 23, 1945, three and a half months after the war with Germany had ended. "The [death] sentence of each accused," he said, "is confirmed and will be carried into execution. . . ."

To the very end, each of the seven young men claimed he had only done his duty. They accepted their sentences calmly, because they knew that there was absolutely

63

The graves of the German submariners at Fort Leavenworth. The simple headstones bear only their names, ranks, and dates of birth and death.

nothing more they could do. Gunther Kuelsen expressed the feelings of all of them in a letter he wrote to his family on the last day of his life: "One can't tie any bonds with the powers of fate."

At midnight on August 25, 1945, the seven German submariners were led, one at a time, across the courtyard at Fort Leavenworth to a gallows, where each was hanged. The entire execution took less than three hours. It was the largest execution for a single crime in the history of the United States.

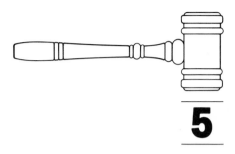

5

Private Eddie Slovik

During the early 1930s, when Eddie Slovik was 11 years old, he began stealing things. Eddie Slovik was one of five children, and his family lived in a poor neighborhood in Detroit, Michigan. Like many other people during the depression of the 1930s, Eddie's father was often out of work. Money, food, and other necessities of life were scarce, and Eddie helped out by working part-time in a bakery. Once in a while he would steal a little bread or a little cake, but no one ever caught him at it.

When Eddie was 12 years old, however, he was caught breaking into a factory with several of his friends. Eddie was placed on probation for a year. When Eddie Slovik was 15, he quit school to earn his own living. He worked at various low-paying jobs, taking almost any unskilled work he could find in those days of widespread unemployment. At the age of 17, when he was working as a clerk in a drugstore, he was charged with having cheated his employer out of some money and with having stolen several items from the store. He was sentenced to 6 months to 10 years confinement and sent off to the state reform school. After serving 9 months of his sentence, Eddie Slovik was paroled and placed on probation. But less than a year after he was released, Eddie and some of his friends stole a car and wrecked it. Eddie escaped arrest, but he turned himself in to the police the next morning. This time he was sentenced to 2-1/2 to 7-1/2 years at the state reformatory.

World War II began while Eddie Slovik was still in prison. By the time he was released, in April 1942, most of Europe had fallen to the German Army, and England had retreated to the safety of its own shores on the other side of the English Channel. The United States Navy had been bombed at Pearl Harbor, and the war was not going well at all for the U. S. armed forces elsewhere in the Pacific. The fighting was intense on all fronts, and the United States was totally committed to one overriding purpose: to fight and win the war. But not every young American male was being drafted to serve in the armed forces. For a variety of reasons, many young men were qualified 4-F: "unfit for military service." Because of his criminal record, Eddie Slovik was one of these young men.

After he was released from the reformatory, Eddie Slovik met a girl. She was crippled and five years older than he was, but Eddie fell in love with her almost immediately. He worked hard at a job that she had found for him, and, most important, he stayed out of trouble. Eddie Slovik and his girl were married in November 1942, just as the United States was landing its first troops in North Africa.

The first year of their marriage was a good one. Eddie

and his wife worked hard, saved their money, and bought a car and some furniture. His wife became pregnant and they were both delighted. The war seemed very far away. On November 7, 1943, the day of the Slovik's first wedding anniversary, Eddie received a letter from the government, notifying him that his classification might be changed to 1-A, which would make him eligible for military service.

The reason for the change was simply that, after nearly two years of war, the country needed more soldiers. The armed forces needed replacements for those who had already been killed or wounded on the battlefields of Europe and Asia. Therefore, the government was lowering its standards for draftees, and thousands of men who had previously been classified 4-F were called in for new physical examinations. And the standards were now much lower. In the words of one author, the new attitude toward physical examinations could be summed up as: "Don't examine his eyes; count them!" Needless to say, Eddie Slovik passed his physical exam. On December 22, 1943, he received the form letter from the government that began with these familiar words: "Greetings. . . you are hereby notified that you have now been selected for training and service [in the land or naval forces of the United States.]" On January 24, 1944, Eddie Slovik became another of the 16,000,000 Americans who were to serve in the United States armed forces during World War II.

Eddie Slovik was not at all happy about the turn of events in his life. He felt that if the United States government was going to draft him they should have done so as soon as he had gotten out of jail. Now he would have to leave a decent job, a happy home, and a pregnant wife, and he felt that was unjust.

Eddie Slovik was not going to get much sympathy for his attitude. After all, more than 10,000,000 young men were drafted in World War II, many with families of their own whom they had left just as reluctantly. They had been drafted because they had stayed out of trouble when they were young, while Eddie Slovik had so far been able to avoid military service because he had broken the law and gone to jail. Eddie was unhappy with his situation, but there was nothing he could do about it (without breaking the law). So Eddie reluctantly got on a train for Camp Wolters, Texas, where he would begin his basic training.

About a month after Eddie Slovik entered the Army, he learned from a friend that his wife had had a miscarriage and was quite ill. He appealed to the Red Cross to obtain a hardship discharge for him, but it was not granted. A few months later, Eddie went home to Detroit on a two-week leave. The weather was warm and sunny, and he was home again, at least for a while. It should have been a joyful time, but he knew that soon he would be going overseas to fight in Europe. Eddie was anything but joyful. In early August 1944, Eddie Slovik boarded a troop transport ship for England. From there, it was only a short boat ride to the battlefields of France.

Private Eddie Slovik was assigned to the 109th Infantry of the 28th Division, a unit whose honored history went all the way back to the days before the American Revolution. On August 25, 1944, he and 11 other replacements landed on the coast of France and set out by truck to catch up with their division. The 28th was about

Private Eddie Slovik

75 miles northeast of Paris, in the thick of the fighting. On the way to join his unit, Eddie got his first glimpse of the horrors of war: the dead bodies of men and animals, the ruined vehicles, and the bombed-out houses. Soon he was in the midst of the war himself. Before he and his companions could reach their division, they were caught

in a barrage of artillery fire and were forced to abandon their truck.

When the shelling was over, the men had gotten separated. Nine of the replacements made their way on foot to join their division. Eddie Slovik and Private John Tankey had become separated from the others and were unable to find either their companions or the unit they were assigned to. So they linked up with a Canadian tank corps and fought with them for the next month and a half. During this time, they sent a letter to their division explaining that they had gotten lost and were trying tò make their way back to their assigned unit. They finally caught up with the 28th Division on October 8th, in the small town of Elsenborn, Belgium. This was where Eddie Slovik's real troubles began.

Eddie Slovik had not wanted to fight in the Army from the day he was drafted, and he still felt bitter about having been forced to leave his home. He missed his wife very deeply; during the seven months he had been in the Army he had written her an average of almost two letters a day. Eddie Slovik did not want to go into combat simply because he did not want to be killed. All he wanted was to be back in Detroit with his beloved wife.

When Tankey and Slovik reported to the company commander of their unit, Eddie said that he did not intend to go into combat. Then he turned and began to walk away. His friend Tankey tried to persuade him to come back, explaining that he could be charged with desertion if he did not. But Eddie refused.

The next day, Eddie Slovik turned himself in to the military police and handed them the following handwritten confession:

I, Pvt. Eddie D. Slovik #36896415, confess to the Desertion of the United States Army. At the time of my Desertion we were in Albuff in France. . . . They were shelling the town, and we were told to dig in for the night. The following morning they were shelling us again. I was so scared nerves and trembling that at the time the other Replacements moved out I couldn't move. . . . I told my commanding officer my story. I said that if I had to go out their again I'd run away. He said their was nothing he could do for me so I ran away again and I'll run away again if I have to go out their.

(Signed) Pvt. Eddie D. Slovik

Eddie Slovik had made his choice. He would rather go to jail than go into combat. And jail is precisely where he was sent. Eddie was confined in the Army stockade at Rocherath, Belgium.

A little more than a month later, on November 11, 1944, Eddie Slovik was brought before a court-martial board in a small town in occupied Germany. Colonel Guy M. Williams was the presiding officer and the board itself was composed of eight other lower-ranking officers. Eddie was charged with two counts of "desertion to avoid hazardous duty." He pleaded "not guilty" to both charges.

The prosecution called five witnesses who simply testified to the bare facts that Eddie Slovik did not join his company with the other replacements, that he deserted a second time when finally he did link up with his company, and that he signed a written confession admitting those acts. His confession was also introduced as evidence. Eddie was told that he had the choice of testifying under oath in his own defense, of making an unsworn statement, or of remaining silent. "I will remain silent," he replied. That statement was the total defense in the case of Eddie Slovik. The court-martial had taken a total of only one hour and 40 minutes.

The court-martial board was unanimous in finding Eddie Slovik guilty as charged. Colonel Williams read the sentence: "To be dishonorably discharged from the service, to forfeit all pay and allowances due or to become due, and to be shot to death with musketry." The sentence seemed severe, but at the time there was good reason to assume that it was really not as bad as it appeared. No member of the American military forces had been executed for desertion since the time of the Civil War. It appeared highly unlikely that Eddie Slovik's death sentence would ever be carried out. There had been similar sentences in previous wars, but they had never been carried out either.

The court-martial board had not known about Eddie Slovik's previous criminal record. His past had not influenced their findings or the sentence in his case. But in any case involving the death penalty, a review of the case was required by armed forces regulations. As a part of the review, the Federal Bureau of Investigation forwarded a copy of Slovik's criminal record to Major General Norman D. Cota, the commander of the 28th Division.

General Cota was a tough, strong-minded professional soldier. For 28 years, from the time of his college days at West Point, the Army had been General Cota's entire life. He had led his troops into North Africa, onto the coast of France on D-Day, and through the rugged fighting in the interior of France and Germany. The

Major General
Norman D. Cota

general was not the type of man who would be likely to have sympathy for a deserter. When he reviewed Slovik's case, General Cota wrote that "only so much of the sentence as provides that the accused be shot to death with musketry is approved. . . ." Officially, at least, Private Eddie Slovik was still condemned to die.

When Slovik learned that his first review had been unsuccessful, he became worried. Eddie Slovik did not want to die. That is why, in fact, he had deserted in the first place: he simply had not wanted to risk getting killed. He preferred to go to jail, and thought that that would be the extent of his punishment. But Eddie's plan was not working out the way he had thought it would. So in December 1944, he composed a long letter to General Dwight D. Eisenhower, supreme commander of all Allied forces in Europe, the man who would be the final authority in the review of his case. Eddie mentioned his civilian record in the letter to Eisenhower, because he was afraid that it might be used against him. "To my knowledge, sir," he added, "I have a good record in the past two years. I also have a good record as a soldier up to the time I got in this trouble."

Eddie explained why he had deserted in much the same way as he had done in his original confession. This time, however, he denied that he had run away the first time, contradicting the statement in his first confession. In desperation, Eddie Slovik pleaded for his life. "How can I tell you," he continued, "how humbley sorry I am for the sins I've committed? I didn't realize at the time what I was doing, or what the word desertion meant. What it is like to be condemned to die. I beg of you deeply and sincerely for the sake of my dear wife and mother back home to have mercy on me. To my knowledge I have a good record since my marriage and as a soldier. I'd like to continue to be a good soldier. [I am] anxiously awaiting your reply, which I earnestly pray is favorable."

Slovik's letter reached General Eisenhower's office on December 12, 1944. It had little or no effect on Eisenhower's decision. On December 23, 1944, an order was issued from Eisenhower's headquarters. "In the foregoing case of Private Eddie D. Slovik," it said, "the sentence, as approved, is confirmed." The order was signed by Eisenhower himself. But although General Eisenhower had confirmed the sentence, Slovik's execution could not be carried out until an opinion was received from the Army's judge advocate general that the trial and the reviews had all been legal and proper.

Two separate legal authorities presented opinions to

In December 1944, General Dwight D. Eisenhower re- viewed Eddie Slovik's case and confirmed the sentence of execution.

General Eisehower regarding the case of Eddie Slovik. One, a judge advocate in Eisenhower's command, noted that Slovik's confession was voluntary and that it left no doubt that Slovik willfully deserted. The judge advocate, however, had also added a rather lengthy section on "clemency," no doubt because clemency had been the rule since the Civil War. "But," he went on to say, "there can be no doubt that [Slovik] deliberately sought the safety and comparative comfort of the guardhouse. To him, and to those soldiers who may follow his example, if he achieves his end, confinement is neither deterrent nor punishment. He has directly challenged the authority of the government, and future discipline depends upon a resolute reply to this challenge." Then, the final recommendation: "If the death penalty is ever to be imposed for desertion it should be imposed in this case, not as a punitive measure nor as a retribution, but to maintain that discipline upon which an army can succeed against the enemy. There was no recommendation for clemency in this case and none is here recommended."

The other legal opinion came from the branch office of the judge advocate in Paris, and it was equally direct. "In this case the extreme penalty of death appears warranted. . . . [Slovik's] unfavorable civilian record indicated that he is not a worthy subject of clemency."

On January 24, 1945, General Cota received the final order. "The sentence having been modified and approved by the convening authority," it said, ". . . will be carried into execution on 31 January 1945. . . by command of General Eisenhower."

The Army decided that the execution of Private Slovik should be carried out away from the eyes of French civilians. Thus, on the morning of January 31, 1945, Private Eddie Slovik was brought to the little town of St. Marie aux Mines, only 20 miles from the German border, where he was to face a firing squad.

The military police turned Slovik over to Army authorities at 7:30 in the morning. He spent the next two and a half hours talking with an Army chaplain and reading a number of letters from his wife that had been saved for him. The time for the execution was drawing near. A military policeman turned to Slovik. "Try to take it easy, Eddie, on yourself—and on us."

"I'm okay," Eddie replied. Then he added, "They're not shooting me for deserting the United States Army— thousands of guys have done that. They're shooting me for the bread I stole when I was 12 years old."

A deep blanket of snow had fallen on St. Marie aux

Eddie Slovik's widow, Antoinette, died on September 7, 1979, a few days before the U. S. Senate was to consider a bill granting her the benefits of her husband's military life insurance.

Mines. At 10 o'clock in the morning, it was quiet and white and very cold. Eddie Slovik was marched through the snow to a brick wall at the end of a garden. There the flag was raised, the order condemning him to death was read, a prayer was said, and he was led to a post that had been planted there especially for him. He was tied to the post, a black hood was placed over his head, and the firing squad marched out into the garden. Twelve young soldiers lined up facing him, and the order to fire was given. Twelve rifles fired in unison, and Eddie Slovik's head slumped forward.

77

Out of the 40,000 American soldiers tried for desertion during World War II, only 49 were actually sentenced to death for their crimes. Private Eddie Slovik, who had wanted to live so much that he defied the Army's rules, was the only man whose sentence was carried out. He was the first person to be executed by the Army for disobeying military orders since the Civil War. Two wars (and more than 30 years) later, no one else has yet become the second.

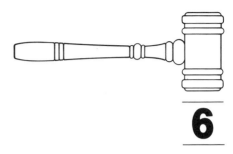

General Tomoyuki Yamashita

By October 1944, World War II was slowly moving toward its close. The war in the Pacific had definitely turned in favor of the United States. The Philippine Islands had been recaptured from the Japanese, and other Pacific strongholds were falling into the hands of the United States. During the battle of Leyte Gulf, at the southern end of the Philippines, Japan lost almost its entire Pacific fleet in the largest sea battle ever fought by the United States.

On October 6, General Tomoyuki Yamashita landed in Manila to assume command of all 250,000 Japanese forces in the Philippines. The Japanese troops stationed there were, for the most part, battle-hardened veterans; as the Allied forces drew near, these Japanese forces prepared to fight. Within two weeks after General Yamashita's arrival, the Philippines came under attack by American armed forces.

General Douglas MacArthur led the American forces

General Douglas MacArthur *(second from right)* returned to the
Philippines in October 1944.

back into the Philippines on October 20, 1944. When the
United States had been forced to surrender the islands
two and a half years earlier, he had uttered the now-
famous words: "I shall return." Now, MacArthur was
returning to fulfill his promise. The battle for control of
the Philippines raged for three months. Although the
Japanese were masters at ambushes and sniper attacks,
and though they used these tactics well in the Philippines,
it soon became clear that the United States was firmly
in command of the military situation there.

Early in the battle for the Philippines, General Yamashita retreated into the mountains on Luzon, the largest

of the Philippine Islands. Some troops had been left in Manila to defend the city, and others had been left in strategic locations to fight the advancing American Army. Yamashita himself set up his well-hidden command post in the densely forested mountains. He hoped to guide his forces from there.

The Japanese soldiers that were left behind, however, did much more than simply fight the Americans. As they retreated, they went on a rampage, murdering Philippine civilians and prisoners of war, raping Philippine women, and looting or simply destroying any of the homes and other buildings that caught their fancy. Tens of thousands of Philippine civilians were killed by the Japanese armed forces in those savage months before the final surrender. It was a senseless and heartless act of violence against the people of the Philippines. The advancing American troops saw what the Japanese soldiers had done, and they were horrified. There was nothing they could do, however, except to push on, hoping to end this horrible carnage by capturing those who were responsible for it.

In February 1945, Manila was captured by American forces. Later that month, the strategic island of Corregidor, which controlled the entrance to Manila Bay, also fell into American hands. For all practical purposes, the Philippines were again under the control of the United States. But General Yamashita and the remainder of his army continued to hide in the mountains of Luzon.

As the months went on, the Japanese Army met with one defeat after another. In August of that year, atomic bombs were dropped on the Japanese cities of Hiroshima and Nagasaki, and the war in the Pacific came to a quick and deadly end. At that point, at the urging of his govern-

Japanese general Tomoyuki Yamashita *(center)* surrenders to American forces on the island of Luzon.

ment, General Yamashita began corresponding with U. S. Army officers to arrange for the surrender of his troops. On September 2, 1945, Japan surrendered formally and unconditionally. That same day, General Yamashita and his troops marched out of hiding and surrendered to the U. S. commander in the Philippines.

But what the Japanese Army had done to the people of the Philippines during those last 10 months was not easily forgotten. The American authorities wanted someone to blame for the Japanese atrocities, and General McArthur personally wanted to insure that the Philippine people were avenged. Since General Yamashita had been in command of the Japanese forces in the Philippines, he was arrested and charged with committing war crimes. According to the formal charges, he had "unlawfully disregarded and failed to discharge his duty as commander to control the operations of the members of his command, permitting them to commit brutal atrocities and other high crimes against the people of the United States and of its allies and dependencies, particularly the Philippines. . . ."

The court-martial of General Yamashita began on October 29, 1945. In those days, the Uniform Code of Military Justice, as we know it today, had not yet been created, and so the rules for the court-martial were set down by General MacArthur. A panel of five very high-ranking officers (three major generals and two brigadier generals) were appointed as the court-martial board, and Army lawyers were appointed to lead the prosecution and the defense. This court-martial would not be an ordinary one. Unlike a normal trial, second-hand, or "hearsay," evidence, rumors, and even opinions were allowed to be presented. The prosecution based its case on showing that the Japanese had committed atrocities against the Philippine people and that General Yamashita, the commander of the Japanese forces, was ultimately responsible for these crimes.

Hundreds of witnesses took the stand and described—often in bloody detail—the crimes that had been committed both against Philippine civilians and against the American prisoners of war who had been held on the islands by the Japanese. Yamashita based his defense on the fact that he had not ordered his troops to do those things, nor had he taken part in them himself. In fact,

General Yamashita on the witness stand

he had not even been aware of what was happening because he had been at his secret command post, completely isolated from the troops on the island. No one, he claimed, had really told him what was going on. "I did not hear at once of the events. . . nor did I have prior knowledge that they might take place," he said. "I put forth my best efforts to control my troops. . . . I feel I did my best." His lawyers also argued that the proceedings of the court-martial itself were unfair and that it therefore should be declared a mistrial.

But the trial continued. After almost six weeks of testimony, the court-martial board reached its decision — "Guilty as charged." The sentence was death by hanging. Immediately, Yamashita's lawyers prepared an appeal. Over the course of the following year, the case of General Yamashita was taken all the way to the United States Supreme Court. The defense lawyers appealed to the Supreme Court on a writ of *habeas corpus*, claiming that Yamashita was being held in prison illegally, because he had been convicted by an illegal court. They claimed that the way in which the court-martial board had been constituted and the procedures followed at the trial had, by their very nature, denied Yamashita the right to due process of law guaranteed by the United States Constitution.

The Court agreed to consider the case, not to determine whether Yamashita was guilty or innocent but because it was concerned about whether his trial had been lawful and, therefore, whether he had been lawfully imprisoned. In February 1946, one and a half years after the Japanese surrendered, the Supreme Court ruled that the trial had been lawful and that the death sentence was valid. Two

General MacArthur refused to issue the order of clemency that would have prevented the execution of General Yamashita.

justices, Frank Murphy and Wiley Rutledge, disagreed strongly and even bitterly with the decision of the majority, but their protests were to no avail. The only hope Yamashita had left was an order of clemency from either General MacArthur or President Harry S Truman. As had been expected, MacArthur refused Yamashita's request for clemency, and President Truman said only that he did not intend to become involved in the case in any way.

On February 23, 1946, General Tomoyuki Yamashita was taken to a small prison outside the city limits of Manila and hanged on the gallows until he died.

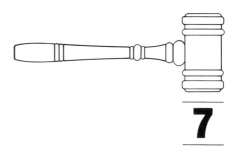

Captain Howard Levy

Howard B. Levy was born and raised in Brooklyn, New York. He grew up in an ordinary Jewish family. Howard was not an exceptional student, but he worked hard in high school and college and finally entered New York University medical school. After graduating from N.Y.U., he began his residency training at Bellevue Hospital in Manhattan, a gigantic public hospital where people are treated if they cannot afford to go to a private hospital. At Bellevue, Howard Levy saw a side of life very different from what he was used to. In the patients there, he saw the hunger, the loneliness, and the suffering of the poor and the unfortunate. The experience had a profound effect on him. He began to feel personally responsible for helping those people who were not getting their fair share in life. He also began to wonder whether the government was really doing all it could to help the people it represented.

Like other young doctors, Howard Levy had been

allowed to finish his medical training, but now he was required to serve in the armed forces. When he reported for duty at Fort Jackson, South Carolina, in July 1965, he experienced a very abrupt and uncomfortable change from the life of a civilian in New York City to the tightly disciplined military life of rural South Carolina.

Because he was a doctor, Levy was automatically assigned the rank of captain. He went to work at the post hospital in his own specialty: dermatology, the branch of medicine concerned with diseases and problems of the skin. But from the day of his arrival at Fort Jackson, Captain Levy knew that he did not like Army life at all. He worked hard as a doctor, but he was not much interested in military routines or rituals of military dress, such as shined shoes, polished brass, and short hair-cuts.

Captain Levy did not participate in the social life at Fort Jackson, because he felt he had nothing in common with the career military officers there. He did not even join the Officer's Club but preferred instead to spend his off-duty hours elsewhere. Instead of socializing with the other officers on the base, Levy became involved in the civil rights movement in South Carolina, especially in helping black people register to vote. Although he was not violating any army regulations, this was not at all the kind of activity that Levy's fellow Army officers approved of. Captain Levy's activities were not interfered with, but he was soon placed under investigation by the Army's Counter-Intelligence Corps.

Captain Levy was unhappy with more than just the Army and the way it was run. He was also disturbed about American military activities in Vietnam. Levy was thoroughly opposed to the nation's participation in that war, and he expressed his opposition quite openly to others in Fort Jackson.

A year before Howard Levy entered the Army, two U. S. Navy ships had been attacked in the Gulf of Tonkin by North Vietnamese gun boats. As a result, Congress gave President Lyndon Johnson the power to send tens of thousands of American troops into Vietnam. Before long, bombing raids over North Vietnam by American planes had become a common event, and American commanders began sending American troops into active combat in South Vietnam. In the United States, this was a time when many people were expressing strong opposition to the war. Some were refusing to go to Vietnam, others were deserting the armed forces, still others were burning their draft cards, and many were demonstrating in the streets of American cities.

Captain Levy was very concerned with the events taking place both in Vietnam and in the United States. At first, he revealed his strong opposition to the Vietnam war only to other members of the hospital staff. After a while, however, he began to argue with other regular Army officers and with enlisted men as well. Because of Levy's work in the civil rights movement and his outspoken opposition to the war in Vietnam, an attachment was placed on his personnel file to signify that he was suspected of being a security risk. His commanding officer was also instructed to be especially watchful of his activities. These measures showed what the Army thought of Captain Levy. One officer claimed that Levy was a "pinko" and a "communist," charges that were never proved against him.

In 1966, some members of the Army's Special Forces,

In the late 1960s, Americans had divided opinions about the Vietnam War. While many participated in protest marches *(above),* others expressed their support of U.S. involvement in the war *(opposite).*

better known as the "Green Berets," were sent to the hospital at Fort Jackson to be given a few days' training in various medical techniques before being shipped to Vietnam. Captain Howard Levy was opposed to training the Green Berets. For one thing, he did not believe it was possible to train a soldier in dermatology for five days to the point where he could do much good. In fact, a partially trained soldier might well do harm. But, more importantly, Levy did not want to do anything to contribute to the United States' military involvement in Vietnam. Training Green Berets to participate actively in the war was, in effect, to participate in the war himself, he said.

At first, Levy did not *instruct* the Green Berets but did allow them to stand around and watch him as he treated his patients. But his conscience continued to bother him. In June 1966, he decided that he had to flatly refuse to have anything to do with training Green Berets. At that point, Levy refused to allow them even to observe him while he was working.

At about this time, a new commanding officer, Colonel Henry F. Fancy, was assigned to the hospital at Fort Jackson. The colonel began to discuss Captain Levy's behavior with the counter-intelligence agent who had been investigating him. Then, in October, Colonel Fancy formally ordered Levy to train the young soldiers who were going to Vietnam. Captain Levy ignored the order, but nothing happened for two months. Then, just before Christmas, the colonel decided that Captain Howard Levy would have to be punished. At first, he chose a mild form of military punishment, used for offenses that are not considered serious enough for a court-martial. Suddenly, however, and for reasons that have never been fully revealed, Colonel Fancy changed his mind and decided instead to bring Levy before a general court-martial, the most serious type of court-martial that can be convened. Levy was charged with refusing to obey the order to train the Green Berets; promoting disloyalty and disaffection among members of the Army; intending to impair the loyalty, morale, and discipline of soldiers he encountered; prejudicing good order and discipline in the armed forces; and conduct unbecoming an officer.

Captain Howard Levy's court-martial began on May 10, 1967, at Fort Jackson. Ten officers were assigned to sit as the court-martial board, and Colonel Earl V. Brown, who had been sent down from Washington, was assigned as the law officer. Levy's defense would be handled by a civilian lawyer named Charles Morgan, who had been provided by the American Civil Liberties Union.

At the beginning of the trial, Morgan made a motion to throw the entire case out of court. He said that the Army was "prosecuting a man for saying it's wrong for the United States to be in Vietnam. What's so wrong about that?" he wanted to know. "U. S. Senators say [the same thing.] We have sergeants going out and speaking for the use of mustard gas in Vietnam. Why can't we have a man speaking against it? I don't think you can prosecute a man for making statements like this." But the

Captain Howard Levy *(left)* with his attorney, Charles Morgan

Army argued that it was not trying to curtail Levy's freedom of speech. In their view, Levy simply did not have the right to try to convince or convert other soldiers to his way of thinking. The court ruled in favor of the Army and denied Morgan's motion to throw out the case.

Colonel Fancy was the chief witness for the prosecution. "I decided to give Captain Levy a direct order to accomplish the training," he testified. "I personally administered the order to Captain Levy . . . [who] then told me that he did not feel he could ethically conduct this training because it was against his principles." During Colonel Fancy's testimony, it was revealed that Captain Levy

93

had previously applied for a discharge from the Army on the grounds that he was a conscientious objector. Several chaplains and a psychiatrist had all recommended that the discharge be granted, but Colonel Fancy had turned down Levy's request.

When the colonel had completed his testimony, several enlisted men who had worked for Captain Levy and 10 Green Berets testified that Levy had spoken against the war in Vietnam and had tried to convert them to his beliefs. A letter that Levy had written to a sergeant in Vietnam was also introduced as evidence. In the letter Levy had suggested that the sergeant should not be fighting the Vietnamese but should rather be back in the United States working for the civil rights movement. After the letter had been presented, the prosecution rested its case.

Defense attorney Charles Morgan then began the case for the defense. First, he brought a number of people to the witness stand to testify that Levy was not "disloyal" to the United States. Morgan wanted to show that the act of expressing opposition to American military policy in Vietnam did not make a person unloyal. In many ways, the witnesses testified, Captain Levy had shown himself to be quite loyal to the United States government both in the past and in the present. Morgan then brought up the question: Did Captain Levy have the right to disobey an order because he believed it to be illegal or immoral? The law officer, Colonel Brown, said that a person did not have the right to disobey an order simply because he believed it to be illegal or improper. He went on to say that if any soldier had that right, the Army would become a debating society rather than a disciplined fighting force. In his opinion, a soldier could only refuse to carry out an order if it directly required him to commit an actual war crime.

The defense decided that, in view of this opinion, it was necessary to show that war crimes *were* being committed in South Vietnam by the Green Berets. The court-martial was then recessed for six days so that the defense could prepare its arguments on this point. When the trial resumed, witnesses who had served in Vietnam testified that war crimes had indeed been committed there, but they had been "directly" committed only by the South Vietnamese forces. There was no evidence that the Green Berets themselves had committed war crimes in that country.

The trial moved on to other issues without having resolved the truly important question of when a soldier has the right to disobey an order. Colonel Brown's legal opinion had established an individual's right to disobey an order to commit a war crime. But it was still not clear whether someone who was *indirectly* involved had the same right of refusal, and that was the real question in the case of Captain Howard Levy.

Captain Levy's lawyer then put several doctors on the witness stand, including Dr. Benjamin Spock, the world-famous baby doctor who was also a strong critic of the war in Vietnam. The doctors took the stand to testify that it was actually against medical ethics for Levy to train the Green Berets. The Green Berets were, first and foremost, soldiers under the control of military and political authorities. Therefore, they were not obliged to abide by medical ethics but only by the wishes of their military and political superiors. The doctors argued that it would not be medically ethical for Howard Levy (or any other doctor) to provide medical training under these circumstances. To do so, they claimed, would be to violate the Hippocratic oath that all doctors take. Finally, the defense maintained that Levy had not, in fact, promoted any disloyalty among the troops. No evidence had been offered to show that Levy had successfully made anyone disloyal. With that final argument, the defense rested its case.

The defense had tried to show that Levy was not part of any effort to undermine the United States government; he was simply opposed to the war in Vietnam and had expressed his opposition publicly. Levy had not obeyed his commander because he believed that it was immoral to do so—that medical ethics made it impossible for him to carry out the order to train the Green Berets. The prosecution, on the other hand, simply said that Levy had refused to obey a *lawful* order, and was therefore guilty and deserving of punishment. The court-martial board of 10 officers agreed with the Army. They found Levy guilty of all charges and sentenced him to three years at hard labor.

Captain Howard Levy began his sentence on June 3, 1967, only one month before he was scheduled to be discharged from the Army. He served out his sentence at Fort Jackson, at the United States Disciplinary Barracks at Fort Leavenworth, Kansas, and at the Federal Penitentiary at Lewisburg, Pennsylvania. During his imprisonment, Levy appealed the sentence, but a decision in his case was never reached. He was finally released from prison in August 1969, after having been imprisoned for over two years.

After his release from prison in 1969, Howard Levy challenged the legality of his court-martial. In 1974, the Supreme Court upheld Levy's conviction.

Both the United States' military involvement in Vietnam and the Vietnamese War itself have now ended, and Captain Howard Levy's case is now just a part of history. His case is, perhaps, important not for the questions it answered but rather for the questions that it *raised* and unfortunately left unanswered.

97

American soldiers in Vietnam prepare a mortar to be fired at enemy positions.

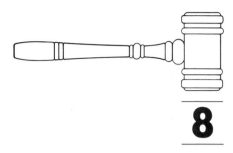

8

Lieutenant William L. Calley

The dreadful story of My Lai started on the morning of March 16, 1968, when American artillery shells began to explode among the scattered grass shacks and small buildings that made up this tiny South Vietnamese village. After the bombardment stopped, U.S. Army helicopters appeared in the sky and then landed quickly in a nearby field. A company of American soldiers scrambled out and, crouching, raced out from under the whirling helicopter blades. The soldiers had expected to be met with fierce armed resistance from the Viet Cong, but instead they were met with nothing but silence. No one was shooting at them, and there were no Viet Cong to be seen anywhere. The soldiers moved quickly toward the village of My Lai.

Commanding the first platoon of soldiers was Lieutenant William L. Calley, a quiet, baby-faced young man who was nicknamed "Rusty" because of his light red hair. As a result of the things that happened in My

Lai that morning, Lieutenant Calley would later stand accused of the mass murder of more than 100 people.

When he entered the village of My Lai in 1968, William Calley had been in the Army for almost two years. Before entering military service, he had tried his hand at many things. Calley had never been a good student. He had graduated from high school almost at the bottom of his class, and he had then flunked out of junior college. Later, Calley took a number of jobs, ranging from railroad conductor to private investigator, but he did not do especially well at these either, and he did not keep any of his jobs for very long.

Finally, late in 1966, William Calley enlisted in the Army and decided to try to become an Army officer. He began his training at officer candidates' school in Fort Benning, Georgia, in March 1967. The school and military training were rugged, and they lasted throughout a seemingly endless spring and summer. When the training period was over, Calley graduated very near the bottom of his class. In other times, when second lieutenants were not in such great demand, Calley might very well have flunked out of the course. But U. S. military involvement in Vietnam was very intense and expanding rapidly at that time, and there was a definite need for new second lieutenants to serve in combat operations. So, in spite of his poor performance in school, Calley was given his second lieutenant's bars and assigned to the 11th Light Infantry Brigade in Hawaii. From there, Calley soon went into combat in Vietnam. On March 16, 1968, Lieutenant William L. Calley, 24 years old, led his platoon in an attack on the village of My Lai.

Many stories would later be told about what happened

in My Lai on that terrible morning, and each story was different from the next. One fact, however, stood out among all the conflicting accounts, a fact disputed by no one. This was that, in spite of the fact that no armed resistance had occurred, almost all the people of My Lai were dead by noon of that day. No one knows exactly how many victims there were, but it has been estimated that more than 400 Vietnamese died in My Lai. All the buildings, houses, and grass shacks in the village had been burned to the ground. All the animals had been killed. American soldiers, who were supposedly fighting in Vietnam to "save" the Vietnamese from their Communist "enemies," had wiped the village of My Lai off the face of the earth.

A report of the mission at My Lai was later written at command headquarters by Lieutenant Colonel Frank A. Barker, and it told quite a different story. "Upon landing," Colonel Barker said in his report, "the rifle companies assault[ed] enemy positions, making a detailed search of all buildings, bunkers, and tunnels." As a result, the report continued, 128 Viet Cong had been killed in action and 11 had been captured. But surprisingly the only enemy equipment reported captured or taken from all those "Viet Cong"—aside from canteens, medical supplies, and so forth—were three rifles, made in the United States. Perhaps to explain why there were no civilians left alive in My Lai after the battle, Colonel Barker ended his report with the following words: ". . . the civilian population supporting the Viet Cong in the area numbered approximately 200. This created a problem in population control and medical care [for] those civilians caught in the fire of the opposing forces. However, the infantry unit on the ground and helicopters were able to assist civilians in leaving the area and in caring for and/or evacuating the wounded."

But the My Lai mission had not happened that way at all. Later, the truth would be revealed, and it would shock the entire world. For the moment, however, the My Lai massacre was quickly covered up and conveniently forgotten.

The war in Vietnam went on, as nasty and ugly as ever. Lieutenant Calley remained in command of his platoon, and he was even promoted to the rank of first lieutenant. His unit continued to fight in Vietnam, conducting assaults on the Viet Cong, search-and-destroy missions, ambushes, patrols, and all the other dangerous business of war. When Calley's tour of duty in Vietnam was over, he volunteered to stay for an additional year and was reassigned to a company of Army Rangers. By then, My Lai had become a thing of the past, and no one really thought much about it anymore. No one, that is, except a soldier named Ronald Ridenhour.

Ridenhour himself had not taken part in the My Lai mission, but he had heard rumors about it, and these rumors aroused his curiosity. He began to ask questions, and the answers he received from some of the men who *had* been there all pointed to one conclusion: some terrible war crimes had been committed at My Lai. Ridenhour gathered as many details as he could, and, when his period of military service was over, he wrote to the Army, to the Department of Defense, and to members of Congress, telling them everything he knew about what had occurred at My Lai. The Army decided to begin investigating Ridenhour's charges. In June 1969, Lieu-

Lieutenant William Calley

tenant William L. Calley received orders to report back
to Washington, D. C., in connection with an Army investigation of the incidents at My Lai.

When he arrived in Washington, Calley was questioned
by Army officers and was told that there was a possibility
he might be charged with murder. He was then sent
to Fort Benning, Georgia, to await the outcome of the
investigation. On September 4, just two days before he

was scheduled to be discharged from the Army, charges were finally filed against Lieutenant William Calley. A formal hearing was scheduled to be held in the office of the judge advocate general at Fort Benning.

The results of the Army investigation soon became known to the public. The story was out in the open now; all the details of the bloody slaughter of women, children, and old people. The outcome of the investigation affected not only those who were present at My Lai but also those who had tried afterwards to cover up the truth. These included several colonels and even the commanding officer of the entire division, Major General Frank Koster. But the central figure in the investigation was Lieutenant William Calley; the massacre had occurred as a result of his actions and the direct orders he had given to others. On November 24, 1969, Calley was formally charged with murder in the first degree. In all, he was accused of having murdered *at least* 102 Vietnamese civilians at My Lai, including women, children, an old priest, and a two-year-old baby.

The general court-martial at which Calley would stand trial for murder was set to begin on November 17, 1970. The court-martial board would be composed of six officers who ranged in rank from colonel down to captain. The law member, who would serve as judge, was Colonel Reid Kennedy, a career Army lawyer. Calley's defense attorney was an experienced civilian lawyer by the name of George Latimer, a specialist in military law. The prosecution was to be led by Captain Aubrey Daniel, who was serving as an Army lawyer after having been drafted. Captain Daniel was only 28 years old. It seemed strange that the Army placed the prosecution of such a tremendously important case in the hands of such a young and inexperienced lawyer. But Aubrey Daniel would prove his worth as an attorney.

In his opening remarks to the court-martial board, Daniel described the story of My Lai in brutal detail. When Calley and his platoon arrived at the village, Aubrey Daniel explained, they found only old men, women, and children, none of them armed. There was no hostile fire. There was no combat. Daniel then told the whole horrible story of how Calley had simply executed unarmed Vietnamese civilians.

When he concluded his opening remarks, Daniel called Ronald Haeberle to testify as one of his first witnesses. Haeberle had not only been at My Lai but he had also taken photographs there. Some of the photographs showed U.S. soldiers, and others showed a large pile of dead bodies in an irrigation ditch, the bodies of some of the Vietnamese who had been killed at My Lai that day. Daniel then called on a number of soldiers who had been involved in the mission but who had not been in Lieutenant Calley's platoon. The soldiers testified that there had been no resistance that day from the Viet Cong, that there had been many dead civilians at the scene, and that Ronald Haeberle's photos had been taken of those same dead civilians.

The next person to testify was an Army helicopter pilot named Hugh Thompson, who had seen the shooting of the Vietnamese civilians, as well as the piles of dead bodies, as he was flying over My Lai. Thompson said that he had immediately landed to demand that Calley stop the slaughter, but that Calley had refused. Thompson then took some of the wounded onto his helicopter and

The village of My Lai is located about 10 miles from the coast, in the northern part of South Vietnam.

flew them out of My Lai. In all, he made three rescue flights that morning, and his passengers were the only villagers from My Lai who survived.

Up to that point in the trial, Captain Daniel had been merely laying the groundwork for the prosecution by establishing that certain war crimes had been committed at My Lai. Now he was proceeding to the next phase, that of establishing that Lieutenant William Calley had committed those crimes. He began by calling the former members of Calley's platoon to the witness stand.

The first witness, Robert Maples, spoke to the jury: "Calley was there at the ditch [where the pile of dead bodies had been photographed]. They had people standing by the hole. Calley and [Private First Class Paul] Meadlo were firing at the people. They were firing into the hole. . . . [Calley] asked me to use my machine gun . . . [but] I refused."

Meadlo himself was to be the next witness, but he refused to testify. Although he had been released from the Army, he was still afraid of what might happen to him for his part in the My Lai massacre. Colonel Kennedy offered to grant Meadlo immunity if he testified; this meant that he could never be prosecuted for any of his testimony in Calley's trial. But Meadlo still refused to talk, and he was turned over to the military police.

The next witness to take the stand was Private Dennis Conti. According to Conti's testimony, Lieutenant Calley had instructed him to round up about six women and children that were nearby. "I brought them back to Calley on the trail. There were others there—30 or 40. All were women and children. I remember one old man. . . ."

"Who was with them?" prosecutor Daniel asked.

"The only G.I. I remember was Meadlo."

"What happened then?"

"Calley told me and Meadlo to take the people off and push them in a rice paddy. We took them out there, pushed them off the trail, and made them squat down and bunch up so they couldn't get up and run. . . ."

"What was Meadlo doing at this time?"

"He was guarding the people," Conti answered.

Daniel asked him what happened after that.

"Lieutenant Calley came out, and said, 'Take care of these people.' So we said, 'okay,' and we stood there and watched them. [Calley] went away, and then he came back and said, 'I thought I told you to take care of these people.' We said, 'We are!' 'No,' he said, 'I mean kill them. . . .' So . . . Calley and Meadlo got on line and fired directly into the people. There were bursts [of fire] and single shots for two minutes. . . . The people screamed and yelled and fell. I guess they tried to get up, too. They couldn't, that was it. The people were pretty well messed up. Lots of heads was shot off, pieces of heads and pieces of flesh flew off the sides and arms. They were all messed up. Meadlo fired a little bit and then broke down. He was crying. . . . He put his weapon into my hands. I said I wouldn't. 'If they're going to be killed, I'm not going to do it. Let Lieutenant Calley do it,' I told him."

The next witness was Charles Sledge, another soldier in Calley's platoon. In the first part of his testimony, he told more or less the same story that Conti had told. But then he added that, after the shooting, he had gone with Calley to meet with Staff Sergeant David Mitchell, who was guarding 20 to 30 more villagers near an irrigation ditch. At first, he said, Calley and Mitchell began only to shove the people into the ditch with their rifles, but then they started shooting them. They continued to fire into the crowd of people in the ditch until they were interrupted by Hugh Thompson, the helicopter pilot. Next, said Sledge, he and Calley approached a Vietnamese priest. "At least I think he was a priest," Sledge said, "because he was dressed in white robes. Lieutenant Calley started to ask him some questions and the priest, he would fold his hands and bow his head . . . and he kept saying 'no Viet.' Then Lieutenant Calley hit him with the butt of his rifle."

"Where did he hit him?" the prosecutor asked.

"Across the mouth; his mouth was bleeding and then he fell back a little and folded his hands, sort of like pleading. Lieutenant Calley took his rifle and point-blank pulled the trigger right in his face and blew half his head off. . . . " After that, Sledge continued, Calley spotted a small Vietnamese child about two years old. He grabbed the child, threw it into a ditch, and shot it.

Private First Class James Dursi then took the witness stand. Dursi had been guarding a different group of villagers from the ones Meadlo and Conti had been guarding. "Calley came to where I was standing with my people, in front of the ditch," Dursi recalled. "Calley came first, and he was followed by Paul Meadlo. Meadlo was all broke up. He was crying. . . . Lieutenant Calley said, 'Meadlo, we've got another job to do. . . . Kill the people in the ditch.' . . . Then Lieutenant Calley gave the order to shoot . . . and [he] and Meadlo started firing into the ditch."

"Did you fire when Lieutenant Calley ordered you to?"

"No. I just stood there. Meadlo turned to me after a couple of minutes and said, 'Shoot! Why don't you shoot? Why don't you fire?' He was crying and yelling. I said, 'I can't; I won't.' And the people were screaming and crying and yelling. . . ."

After this testimony, the prosecution rested its case. Defense counsel George Latimer then began his defense of Lieutenant Calley, but the prosecution interrupted him not long after he began. Something had happened; the prosecution wanted to tell its story one more time. By now, the bloody story had been told so many times that no one really wanted to hear it again. But there was one more witness who had decided to testify. That witness was Paul Meadlo, and everyone wanted to hear what Meadlo had to say.

Meadlo began by describing how he had been guarding some of the villagers, including a number of women and children. "We suspected them of being Viet Cong," he said, "and as far as I'm concerned, they're still Viet Cong. Calley said to me, 'You know what to do with them, Meadlo.' I assumed he wanted me to guard them. That's what I did. But Calley came back later, and said 'How come they're not dead? I want them dead.' Then he backed off 20 or 30 feet and started shooting the people . . . and I helped shoot them."

"How were you feeling at that time?" Daniel asked.

"I was mortally upset; scared . . ."

"Were you crying?"

"I imagine I was."

Meadlo then described how he and Calley had shot another group of civilians in a ditch, as PFC. James Dursi looked on. There may have been as many as 100 villagers in this group, Meadlo said, and he and Calley killed them all.

When Meadlo had finished, prosecutor Daniel asked Meadlo whether Captain Ernest Medina, Calley's commanding officer, had ordered him to kill. "I took my orders from Lieutenant Calley," Meadlo replied, "but Captain Medina was there before the ditch and I assumed everything was okay, because if it wasn't I assumed he would put a stop to it. And he didn't, so I assumed it was right. With all the bodies lying around, why didn't he put a stop to all the killings?" Paul Meadlo was then excused from the witness stand.

Aubrey Daniel had built quite a case, presenting a chilling, terrifying picture of what had happened at My Lai. Throughout the testimony, Lieutenant Calley had simply watched and listened, displaying little emotion. Aubrey Daniel's case for the United States government was over. Soon it would be Calley's turn to testify.

Defense attorney Latimer did not set out to show that no war crimes had taken place at My Lai; that would have been simply impossible, because the evidence of mass murder was overwhelming. Instead, the main thrust of his defense was to show that the murders had been ordered by Calley's commanding officer, Captain Medina. The defense claimed that Calley was simply carrying out orders he believed were just and legal. In effect, Latimer was saying that Captain Medina, not Calley, should have been on trial for murder. Latimer also argued that, because of his mental state, Calley might not have been responsible for his acts on that day. Three psychiatrists testified that this was a distinct possibility. At this point, Colonel Reid Kennedy sent Calley to the Walter

Reed Army Hospital in Washington, D.C., for a complete psychiatric examination. The Army psychiatrists at Walter Reed found Calley to be legally sane, and the defense was allowed to proceed with its case.

It was near the end of February 1971, when Lieutenant Calley took the stand to testify to his own defense. Calley began by saying that he had never been told that he was expected to decide whether an order was legal or not. On the contrary, he had been instructed that, if he questioned an order, he was supposed to carry it out first and then make his complaint later.

Calley then testified that, on the night before the My Lai mission, Captain Medina had ordered the soldiers to attack and destroy the village. Everyone in My Lai was either a member of the Viet Cong or a Viet Cong sympathizer, Medina had said, and all other South Vietnamese civilians had left the area. After his platoon had reached the village, Calley continued, he received a radio call from Captain Medina, who wanted to know what was slowing him down. "Waste the Vietnamese and get my people out in the position they are supposed to be," said Medina. At that point, said Calley, he went over to Private Meadlo: "I told him that if he couldn't move all those people to get rid of them." After that, Calley testified that he had left.

Calley denied that he had shot any of the civilians who had been described in the charges against him. He admitted killing several people that morning, but they were not, he said, the same ones he was charged with having murdered. Calley did not deny that *his men* had shot the civilians, only that Medina had ordered everyone and everything in My Lai destroyed, and, though this order had been carried out to the last detail, Calley himself had not done it.

Calley was staking his own word against the statments of all those who had already testified against him. It was Calley alone against all the rest. He did admit that he struck a Vietnamese man with the butt of his rifle when the man would not answer his questions. But he denied having shot him. At first, he also denied having shot the two-year-old Vietnamese child. Later, however, Calley changed his testimony and admitted killing a small person whom, he claimed, he had not recognized as being a child until after he had pulled the trigger.

Even if the court-martial board did not believe Calley's version of what had happened, Calley still had his other defense: "I was ordered," he said, "to go in there and destroy the enemy. That was my job on that day. That was the mission I was given. I did not sit down and think in terms of men, women, and children. They were all classified the same [as enemy soldiers], and that was the classification that we dealt with. . . . I felt then, and I still do, that I acted as I was directed, and I carried out the orders that I was given, and I do not feel wrong in doing so. . . ."

Prosecutor Daniel cross-examined him at great length and in great detail, but Calley stuck to his story. He testified that he had not even taken part in the incidents described by so many of the men under his command. Then he stepped down from the witness stand, and the defense rested its case.

There was still one more witness to be called, however. His testimony was requested not by the prosecution or the defense but by the court-martial board. This last witness was Captain Ernest Medina. Captain Medina arrived at Fort Benning with F. Lee Bailey (one of the country's most famous criminal lawyers) representing him. Medina was calm and cooperative on the witness stand, but his testimony certainly did not help Calley's case. Medina testified that, according to his information, there were no civilians left in My Lai and that his unit would face strong opposition and fierce fighting when it arrived. But that was about the only thing he and Lieutenant Calley seemed to agree about.

According to Calley, Medina had said at the briefing that their job would be "to go in rapidly and to neutralize everything; to kill everything." Then, according to Calley, someone asked: "Do you mean women and children, too?" and Medina had replied: "I mean everything." But when Medina was asked in court whether someone had raised that question at the briefing, Medina replied that it *had* been raised, but that he had replied, "No, you do *not* kill women and children. You must use common sense. . . ." Medina then denied every other statement that Calley had attributed to him.

"Did you at any time . . . order or direct Lieutenant Calley to kill or 'waste' any Vietnamese people?" Medina was asked.

"No sir," he replied.

Captain Medina told his side of the story in detail, and he was cross-examined by both the prosecution and the defense. But he stuck to his story and did not become rattled even under the flurry of questions. When the cross-examinations were over, Medina was dismissed, and, for all practical purposes, the trial was over. Lieutenant Calley and Captain Medina had told very different stories.

There was additional testimony from others that tended to support Medina's version, and further testimony that tended to support Calley's version. The exact truth may, in fact, never be known.

In his final argument, Aubrey Daniel repeated the highlights of the trial and reminded the jury of all the many witnesses who had testified against Calley. It had been proven, he said, that Calley *did kill*—and *ordered to be killed*—unarmed Vietnamese men, women, and children who were purely civilians. For having done these things, Calley was guilty of murder. Furthermore, Daniel argued, Lieutenant Calley would be guilty even if he had been *ordered* to do these things. Any such order would have been completely illegal, and Calley could not have legally carried it out.

George Latimer based his final argument for the defense on the idea that those who had testified against Calley simply had grudges to bear. He said that the trial was really to decide who should be "killed" for the crimes committed at My Lai: Calley or Medina. Clearly, argued Latimer, it should be Medina; Calley was just a good officer, carrying out his orders.

The court-martial of Lieutenant William L. Calley came to an end on March 16, 1971, three years to the day after Calley had led his troops into My Lai, three years from the time that the entire village and all its inhabitants had been destroyed. Calley's trial, which had lasted four months, was the longest court-martial in American history. The jury of six officers also took a long time to reach a decision. Thirteen days passed before the court-martial board announced its findings: Lieutenant William L. Calley was guilty of the premeditated murder of 22

Lieutenant William Calley is escorted from the courtroom after being found guilty of premeditated murder.

human beings. On the next day, Calley was sentenced to life imprisonment, and he was taken from the courtroom to the stockade at Fort Benning. His only victory, it seemed, was that he had escaped the death penalty. The same could not be said for the people of My Lai.

But Calley was to escape more than the death penalty. The American public seemed to be on his side, and many thought that his sentence was much too harsh. Calley's case became a political issue, and President Richard Nixon decided to intervene. On the president's authority,

Lieutenant Calley was removed from the stockade and instead simply confined to his apartment on the Army base. There, he could live in complete comfort and with a great deal of freedom. His girl friend and others could

The stockade at Fort Benning where Calley was imprisoned after his trial. Later, he was confined to his apartment on the Army base.

visit him, he could eat and drink what he pleased, and he could work (with a professional writer named John Sack) on a book about his experiences, for which he would be paid at least $50,000. In effect, President Nixon had disregarded the outcome of the court-martial and taken the law into his own hands.

In August 1971, President Nixon went even further and reduced Lieutenant Calley's sentence from life to 20 years. Later, the sentence was reduced to 10 years in prison. Finally, on November 19, 1974, after having spent only three and a half years in custody in his own apartment, William Calley was paroled and set free.

The legal proceedings have now ended in the case of William Calley, and the ordeal has ended for all the others involved in the My Lai massacre. The memory and shame of My Lai, however, will be a part of American history forever.

Index

military law, 5-7
Milligan, Lambdin P.: arrest of,
10, 13; background of, 10; case
of, heard by Supreme Court,
18-20; court-martial of, 13-14
Mitchell, Billy: court-martial of,
41-47; death of, 47, 48;
demonstration of air power
staged by, 35, 37, 39; experience
of, in World War I, 37
Mitchell, David, 108-109
Morgan, Charles, 92-93, 94-95
Murphy, Frank, 86
Murza, Friedrich, 53-55
My Lai, 105, 107, 111, 112, 114,
116, 118; attack on, 99-101;
investigation of attack on,
102-103, 104; number of
civilians killed at, 100, 101, 104,
115-116

Nagasaki, 48, 81
Navy, U.S., 37, 39-40, 44-45,
47-48, 51
Nixon, Richard, 116-118

Ostfriesland, 35, 39

Papago Park, Ariz., POW camp
at, 52
Pearl Harbor, attack on, 48, 66
Philippine Islands, 79-81, 83

Reid, Frank R., 41-42, 44
Reyak, Bernhard, 54
Rickenbacker, Eddie, 42
Ridenhour, Ronald, 102
Rogers, Will, 42
Rutledge, Wiley, 86

Schmidt, Oscar, 58, 59
Schofield, John M., 24, 26, 29,
30-31
Shedd, William E., 61
Shenandoah, 39-41, 44-45
Sledge, Charles, 108-109
Slovik, Eddie: background of,
65-67; confession of, 71; court-
martial of, 71-72; execution of,
77-78; experience of, in battle,
69-70
Sons of Liberty, 12
special court-martial, definition
of, 6
Spock, Benjamin, 95

Stengel, Otto, 54, 58-59
Stockton, Calif., secret camp at,
53, 55, 58
submariners, seven German:
appeal of, 61; capture of, 50;
confession of, 54, 55; court-
martial of, 55-59, 61; execution
of, 64; names of, 54
summary court-martial, definition
of, 6
Summerall, Charles P., 41-42
Supreme Court, U.S., 15, 16-20,
85-86
Swain, D.G., 33

Taney, Roger B., 16-17
Tankey, John, 70
Taylor (defense attorney for
German submariners), 58, 59
Thompson, Hugh, 105, 107, 109
Truman, Harry S, 63, 86
28th Division (U.S. Army), 68-69,
70, 72

Uniform Code of Military Justice,
83
Union Army, 11, 12, 13

Viet Cong, 99, 101, 112
Vietnam war, 48, 88-89, 90, 97,
100, 102; opposition to, 89, 92,
94; war crimes during, 95, 102,
107, 111

Wattenburg, Jurgen, 53
West Point, U.S. Military
Academy at, 26, 29, 30; black
cadets at, 23; graduates of, 21;
traditions of, 21, 23, 31
Whittaker, Johnson: attack on,
23-25; background of, 21, 23;
court-martial of, 30-32; court of
inquiry for, 27-29, 32; discharge
of, from West Point, 34;
treatment of, at West Point, 23
Williams, Guy M., 71, 72
Wizuy, Rolf, 54, 59
World War I, 7, 34, 35, 37
World War II, 49, 62-63, 66, 67,
68; battles of, in Pacific, 66,
79-81, 83

Yamashita, Tomoyuki, 79, 80-81;
court-martial of, 83-85;
execution of, 86; surrender of,
83

120